George Bernard Shaw

By G. K. Chesterton

NEW YORK: JOHN LANE COMPANY MCMX

* * * *

* * * *

Introduction to the First Edition

MOST people either say that they agree with Bernard Shaw or that they do not understand him. I am the only person who understands him, and I do not agree with him.

G. K. C.

The Problem of a Preface

A PECULIAR difficulty arrests the writer of this rough study at the very start. Many people know Mr. Bernard Shaw chiefly as a man who would write a very long preface even to a very short play. And there is truth in the idea; he is indeed a very prefatory sort of person. He always gives the explanation before the incident; but so, for the matter of that, does the Gospel of St. John. For Bernard Shaw, as for the mystics, Christian and heathen (and Shaw is best described as a heathen mystic), the philosophy of facts is anterior to the facts themselves. In due time we come to the fact, the incarnation; but in the beginning was the Word.

This produces upon many minds an impression of needless preparation and a kind of bustling prolixity. But the truth is that the very rapidity of such a man's mind makes him seem slow in getting to the point. It is positively because he is quick-witted that he is long-winded. A quick eye for ideas may actually make a writer slow in reaching his goal, just as a quick eye for landscapes might make a motorist slow in reaching Brighton. An original man has to pause at every allusion or simile to re-explain historical parallels, to re-shape distorted words. Any ordinary leader-writer (let us say) might write swiftly and smoothly something like this: "The element of religion in the Puritan rebellion, if hostile to art, yet saved the movement from some of the evils in which the French Revolution involved morality." Now a man like Mr. Shaw, who has his own views on everything, would be forced to make the sentence long and broken instead of swift and smooth. He would say something like: "The element of religion, as I explain religion, in the Puritan rebellion (which you wholly misunderstand) if hostile to art--that is what I mean by art-- may have saved it from some evils (remember my definition of evil) in which the French Revolution--of which I have my own opinion-- involved morality, which I will define for you in a minute." That is the worst of being a really universal sceptic and philosopher; it is such slow work. The very forest of the man's thoughts chokes up his thoroughfare. A man must be orthodox upon most things, or he will never even have time to preach his own heresy.

Now the same difficulty which affects the work of Bernard Shaw affects also any book about him. There is an unavoidable artistic necessity to put the preface before the play; that is, there is a necessity to say something of what Bernard Shaw's experience means before one even says what it was. We have to mention what he did when we have already explained why he did it. Viewed superficially, his life consists of fairly conventional incidents, and might easily fall under fairly conventional phrases. It might be the life of any Dublin clerk or Manchester Socialist or London author. If I touch on the man's life before his work, it will seem trivial; yet taken with his work it is most important. In short, one could scarcely know what Shaw's doings meant unless one knew what he meant by them. This difficulty in mere order and construction has puzzled me very much. I am going to overcome it, clumsily perhaps, but in the way which affects me as most sincere. Before I write even a slight suggestion of his relation to the stage, I am going to write of three soils or atmospheres out of which that relation grew. In other words, before I write of Shaw I will write of the three great influences upon Shaw. They were all three there before he was born, yet each one of them is himself and a very vivid portrait of him from one point of view. I have called these three traditions: "The Irishman," "The Puritan," and "The Progressive." I do not see how this prefatory theorising is to be avoided; for if I simply said, for instance, that Bernard Shaw was an Irishman, the impression produced on the reader might be remote from my thought and, what is more important, from Shaw's. People might think, for instance, that I meant that he was "irresponsible." That would throw out the whole plan of these pages, for if there is one thing that Shaw is not, it is irresponsible. The responsibility in him rings like steel. Or, again, if I simply called him a Puritan, it might mean something about nude statues or "prudes on the prowl." Or if I called him a Progressive, it might be supposed to mean that he votes for Progressives at the County Council election, which I very much doubt. I have no other course but this: of briefly explaining such matters as Shaw himself might explain them. Some fastidious persons may object to my thus putting the moral in front of the fable. Some may imagine in their innocence that they already understand the word Puritan or the yet more mysterious word Irishman. The only person, indeed, of whose approval I feel fairly certain is Mr. Bernard Shaw himself, the man of many introductions.

CONTENTS

* * * *

The Irishman

THE English public has commonly professed, with a kind of pride, that it cannot understand Mr. Bernard Shaw. There are many reasons for it which ought to be adequately considered in such a book as this. But the first and most obvious reason is the mere statement that George Bernard Shaw was born in Dublin in 1856. At least one reason why Englishmen cannot understand Mr. Shaw is that Englishmen have never taken the trouble to understand Irishmen. They will sometimes be generous to Ireland; but never just to Ireland. They will speak to Ireland; they will speak for Ireland; but they will not hear Ireland speak. All the real amiability which most Englishmen undoubtedly feel towards Irishmen is lavished upon a class of Irishmen which unfortunately does not exist. The Irishman of the English farce, with his brogue, his buoyancy, and his tender-hearted irresponsibility, is a man who ought to have been thoroughly pampered with praise and sympathy, if he had only existed to receive them. Unfortunately, all the time that we were creating a comic Irishman in fiction, we were creating a tragic Irishman in fact. Never perhaps has there been a situation of such excruciating cross-purposes even in the three-act farce. The more we saw in the Irishman a sort of warm and weak fidelity, the more he regarded us with a sort of icy anger. The more the oppressor looked down with an amiable pity, the more did the oppressed look down with a somewhat unamiable contempt. But, indeed, it is needless to say that such comic cross-purposes could be put into a play; they have been put into a play. They have been put into what is perhaps the most real of Mr. Bernard Shaw's plays, John Bull's Other Island.

It is somewhat absurd to imagine that any one who has not read a play by Mr. Shaw will be reading a book about him. But if it comes to that it is (as I clearly perceive) absurd to be writing a book about Mr. Bernard Shaw at all. It is indefensibly foolish to attempt to explain a man whose whole object through life has been to explain himself. But even in nonsense there is a need for logic and consistency; therefore let us proceed on the assumption that when I say that all Mr. Shaw's blood and origin may be found in John Bull's Other Island, some reader may answer that he does not know the play. Besides, it is more important to put the reader right about England and Ireland even than to put him right about Shaw. If he reminds me that this is a book about Shaw, I can only assure him that I will reasonably, and at proper intervals, remember the fact.

Mr. Shaw himself said once, "I am a typical Irishman; my family came from Yorkshire." Scarcely anyone but a typical Irishman could have made the remark. It is in fact a bull, a conscious bull. A bull is only a paradox which people are too stupid to understand. It is the rapid summary of something which is at once so true and so complex that the speaker who has the swift intelligence to perceive it, has not the slow patience to explain it. Mystical dogmas are much of this kind. Dogmas are often spoken of as if they were signs of the slowness or endurance of the human mind. As a matter of fact, they are marks of mental promptitude and lucid impatience. A man will put his meaning mystically because he cannot waste time in putting it rationally. Dogmas are not dark and mysterious; rather a dogma is like a flash of lightning--an instantaneous lucidity that opens across a whole landscape. Of the same nature are Irish bulls; they are summaries which are too true to be consistent. The Irish make Irish bulls for the same reason that they accept Papal bulls. It is because it is better to speak wisdom foolishly, like the Saints, rather than to speak folly wisely, like the Dons.

This is the truth about mystical dogmas and the truth about Irish bulls; it is also the truth about the paradoxes of Bernard Shaw. Each of them is an argument impatiently shortened into an epigram. Each of them represents a truth hammered and hardened, with an almost disdainful violence until it is compressed into a small space, until it is made brief and almost incomprehensible. The case of that curt remark about Ireland and Yorkshire is a very typical one. If Mr. Shaw had really attempted to set out all the sensible stages of his joke, the sentence would have run something like this: "That I am an Irishman is a fact of psychology which I can trace in many of the things that come out of me, my fastidiousness, my frigid fierceness and my distrust of mere pleasure. But the thing must be tested by what comes from me; do not try on me the dodge of asking where I came from, how many batches of three hundred and sixty-five days my family was in Ireland. Do not play any games on me about whether I am a Celt, a word that is dim to the anthropologist and utterly unmeaning to anybody else. Do not start any drivelling discussions about whether the word Shaw is German or Scandinavian or Iberian or Basque. You know you are human; I know I am Irish. I know I belong to a certain type and temper of society; and I know that all sorts of people of all sorts of blood live in that society and by that society; and are therefore Irish. You can take your books of anthropology to hell or to Oxford." Thus gently, elaborately and at length, Mr. Shaw would have explained his meaning, if he had thought it worth his while. As he did not he merely flung the symbolic, but very complete sentence, "I am a typical Irishman; my family came from Yorkshire."

What then is the colour of this Irish society of which Bernard Shaw, with all his individual oddity, is yet an essential type? One generalisation, I think, may at least be made. Ireland has in it a quality which caused it (in the most ascetic age of Christianity) to be called the "Land of Saints"; and which still might give it a claim to be called the Land of Virgins. An Irish Catholic priest once said to me, "There is in our people a fear of the passions which is older even than Christianity." Everyone who has read Shaw's play upon Ireland will remember the thing in the horror of the Irish girl at being kissed in the public streets. But anyone who knows Shaw's work will recognize it in Shaw himself. There exists by accident an early and beardless portrait of him which really suggests in the severity and purity of its lines some of the early ascetic pictures of the beardless Christ. However he may shout profanities or seek to shatter the shrines, there is always something about him which suggests that in a sweeter and more solid civilisation he would have been a great saint. He would have been a saint of a sternly ascetic, perhaps of a sternly negative type. But he has this strange note of the saint in him: that he is literally unworldly. Worldliness has no human magic for him; he is not bewitched by rank nor drawn on by conviviality at all. He could not understand the intellectual surrender of the snob. He is perhaps a defective character; but he is not a mixed one. All the virtues he has are heroic virtues. Shaw is like the Venus of Milo; all that there is of him is admirable.

But in any case this Irish innocence is peculiar and fundamental in him; and strange as it may sound, I think that his innocence has a great deal to do with his suggestions of sexual revolution. Such a man is comparatively audacious in theory because he is comparatively clean in thought. Powerful men who have powerful passions use much of their strength in forging chains for themselves; they alone know how strong the chains need to be. But there are other souls who walk the woods like Diana, with a sort of wild chastity. I confess I think that this Irish purity a little disables a critic in dealing, as Mr. Shaw has dealt, with the roots and reality of the marriage law. He forgets that those fierce and elementary functions which drive the universe have an impetus which goes beyond itself and cannot always easily be recovered. So the healthiest men may often erect a law to watch them, just as the healthiest sleepers may want an alarum clock to wake them up. However this may be, Bernard Shaw certainly has all the virtues and all the powers that go with this original quality in Ireland. One of them is a sort of awful elegance; a dangerous and somewhat inhuman daintiness of taste which sometimes seems to shrink from matter itself, as though it were mud. Of the many sincere things Mr. Shaw has said he never said a more sincere one than when he stated he was a vegetarian, not because eating meat was bad morality, but because it was bad taste. It would be fanciful to say that Mr. Shaw is a vegetarian because he comes of a race of vegetarians, of peasants who are compelled to accept the simple life in the shape of potatoes. But I am sure that his fierce fastidiousness in such matters is one of the allotropic forms of the Irish purity; it is to the virtue of Father Matthew what a coal is to a diamond. It has, of course, the quality common to all special and unbalanced types of virtue, that you never know where it will stop. I can feel what Mr. Shaw probably means when he says that it is disgusting to feast off dead bodies, or to cut lumps off what was once a living thing. But I can never know at what moment he may not feel in the same way that it is disgusting to mutilate a pear-tree, or to root out of the earth those miserable mandrakes which cannot even groan. There is no natural limit to this rush and riotous gallop of refinement.

But it is not this physical and fantastic purity which I should chiefly count among the legacies of the old Irish morality. A much more important gift is that which all the saints declared to be the reward of chastity: a queer clearness of the intellect, like the hard clearness of a crystal. This certainly Mr. Shaw possesses; in such degree that at certain times the hardness seems rather clearer than the clearness. But so it does in all the most typical Irish characters and Irish attitudes of mind. This is probably why Irishmen succeed so much in such professions as require a certain crystalline realism, especially about results. Such professions are the soldier and the lawyer; these give ample opportunity for crimes but not much for mere illusions. If you have composed a bad opera you may persuade yourself that it is a good one; if you have carved a bad statue you can think yourself better than Michael Angelo. But if you have lost a battle you cannot believe you have won it; if your client is hanged you cannot pretend that you have got him off.

There must be some sense in every popular prejudice, even about foreigners. And the English people certainly have somehow got an impression and a tradition that the Irishman is genial, unreasonable, and sentimental. This legend of the tender, irresponsible Paddy has two roots; there are two elements in the Irish which made the mistake possible. First, the very logic of the Irishman makes him regard war or revolution as extra-logical, an ultima ratio which is beyond reason. When fighting a powerful enemy he no more worries whether all his charges are exact or all his attitudes dignified than a soldier worries whether a cannon-ball is shapely or a plan of campaign picturesque. He is aggressive; he attacks. He seems merely to be rowdy in Ireland when he is really carrying the war into Africa--or England. A Dublin tradesman printed his name and trade in archaic Erse on his cart. He knew that hardly anybody could read it; he did it to annoy. In his position I think he was quite right. When one is oppressed it is a mark of chivalry to hurt oneself in order to hurt the oppressor. But the English (never having had a real revolution since the Middle Ages) find it very hard to understand this steady passion for being a nuisance, and mistake it for mere whimsical impulsiveness and folly. When an Irish member holds up the whole business of the House of Commons by talking of his bleeding country for five or six hours, the simple English members suppose that he is a sentimentalist. The truth is that he is a scornful realist who alone remains unaffected by the sentimentalism of the House of Commons. The Irishman is neither poet enough nor snob enough to be swept away by those smooth social and historical tides and tendencies which carry Radicals and Labour members comfortably off their feet. He goes on asking for a thing because he wants it; and he tries really to hurt his enemies because they are his enemies. This is the first of the queer confusions which make the hard Irishman look soft. He seems to us wild and unreasonable because he is really much too reasonable to be anything but fierce when he is fighting.

In all this it will not be difficult to see the Irishman in Bernard Shaw. Though personally one of the kindest men in the world, he has often written really in order to hurt; not because he hated any particular men (he is hardly hot and animal enough for that), but because he really hated certain ideas even unto slaying. He provokes; he will not let people alone. One might even say that he bullies, only that this would be unfair, because he always wishes the other man to hit back. At least he always challenges, like a true Green Islander. An even stronger instance of this national trait can be found in another eminent Irishman, Oscar Wilde. His philosophy (which was vile) was a philosophy of ease, of acceptance, and luxurious illusion; yet, being Irish, he could not help putting it in pugnacious and propagandist epigrams. He preached his softness with hard decision; he praised pleasure in the words most calculated to give pain. This armed insolence, which was the noblest thing about him, was also the Irish thing; he challenged all comers. It is a good instance of how right popular tradition is even when it is most wrong, that the English have perceived and preserved this essential trait of Ireland in a proverbial phrase. It is true that the Irishman says, "Who will tread on the tail of my coat?"

But there is a second cause which creates the English fallacy that the Irish are weak and emotional. This again springs from the very fact that the Irish are lucid and logical. For being logical they strictly separate poetry from prose; and as in prose they are strictly prosaic, so in poetry they are purely poetical. In this, as in one or two other things, they resemble the French, who make their gardens beautiful because they are gardens, but their fields ugly because they are only fields. An Irishman may like romance, but he will say, to use a frequent Shavian phrase, that it is "only romance." A great part of the English energy in fiction arises from the very fact that their fiction half deceives them. If Rudyard Kipling, for instance, had written his short stories in France, they would have been praised as cool, clever little works of art, rather cruel, and very nervous and feminine; Kipling's short stories would have been appreciated like Maupassant's short stories. In England they were not appreciated but believed. They were taken seriously by a startled nation as a true picture of the empire and the universe. The English people made haste to abandon England in favour of Mr. Kipling and his imaginary colonies; they made haste to abandon Christianity in favour of Mr. Kipling's rather morbid version of Judaism. Such a moral boom of a book would be almost impossible in Ireland, because the Irish mind distinguishes between life and literature. Mr. Bernard Shaw himself summed this up as he sums up so many things in a compact sentence which he uttered in conversation with the present writer, "An Irishman has two eyes." He meant that with one eye an Irishman saw that a dream was inspiring, bewitching, or sublime, and with the other eye that after all it was a dream. Both the humour and the sentiment of an Englishman cause him to wink the other eye. Two other small examples will illustrate the English mistake. Take, for instance, that noble survival from a nobler age of politics--I mean Irish oratory. The English imagine that Irish politicians are so hot-headed and poetical that they have to pour out a torrent of burning words. The truth is that the Irish are so clear-headed and critical that they still regard rhetoric as a distinct art, as the ancients did. Thus a man makes a speech as a man plays a violin, not necessarily without feeling, but chiefly because he knows how to do it. Another instance of the same thing is that quality which is always called the Irish charm. The Irish are agreeable, not because they are particularly emotional, but because they are very highly civilised. Blarney is a ritual; as much of a ritual as kissing the Blarney Stone.

Lastly, there is one general truth about Ireland which may very well have influenced Bernard Shaw from the first; and almost certainly influenced him for good. Ireland is a country in which the political conflicts are at least genuine; they are about something. They are about patriotism, about religion, or about money: the three great realities. In other words, they are concerned with what commonwealth a man lives in or with what universe a man lives in or with how he is to manage to live in either. But they are not concerned with which of two wealthy cousins in the same governing class shall be allowed to bring in the same Parish Councils Bill; there is no party system in Ireland. The party system in England is an enormous and most efficient machine for preventing political conflicts. The party system is arranged on the same principle as a three-legged race: the principle that union is not always strength and is never activity. Nobody asks for what he really wants. But in Ireland the loyalist is just as ready to throw over the King as the Fenian to throw over Mr. Gladstone; each will throw over anything except the thing that he wants. Hence it happens that even the follies or the frauds of Irish politics are more genuine as symptoms and more honourable as symbols than the lumbering hypocrisies of the prosperous Parliamentarian. The very lies of Dublin and Belfast are truer than the truisms of Westminster. They have an object; they refer to a state of things. There was more honesty, in the sense of actuality, about Piggott's letters than about the Times' leading articles on them. When Parnell said calmly before the Royal Commission that he had made a certain remark "in order to mislead the House" he proved himself to be one of the few truthful men of his time. An ordinary British statesman would never have made the confession, because he would have grown quite accustomed to committing the crime. The party system itself implies a habit of stating something other than the actual truth. A Leader of the House means a Misleader of the House.

Bernard Shaw was born outside all this; and he carries that freedom upon his face. Whether what he heard in boyhood was violent Nationalism or virulent Unionism, it was at least something which wanted a certain principle to be in force, not a certain clique to be in office. Of him the great Gilbertian generalisation is untrue; he was not born either a little Liberal or else a little Conservative. He did not, like most of us, pass through the stage of being a good party man on his way to the difficult business of being a good man. He came to stare at our general elections as a Red Indian might stare at the Oxford and Cambridge boat-race, blind to all its irrelevant sentimentalities and to some of its legitimate sentiments. Bernard Shaw entered England as an alien, as an invader, as a conqueror. In other words, he entered England as an Irishman.

* * * *

The Puritan

IT has been said in the first section that Bernard Shaw draws from his own nation two unquestionable qualities, a kind of intellectual chastity, and the fighting spirit. He is so much of an idealist about his ideals that he can be a ruthless realist in his methods. His soul has (in short) the virginity and the violence of Ireland. But Bernard Shaw is not merely an Irishman; he is not even a typical one. He is a certain separated and peculiar kind of Irishman, which is not easy to describe. Some Nationalist Irishmen have referred to him contemptuously as a "West Briton." But this is really unfair; for whatever Mr. Shaw's mental faults may be, the easy adoption of an unmeaning phrase like "Briton" is certainly not one of them. It would be much nearer the truth to put the thing in the bold and bald terms of the old Irish song, and to call him "The anti-Irish Irishman." But it is only fair to say that the description is far less of a monstrosity than the anti-English Englishman would be; because the Irish are so much stronger in self-criticism. Compared with the constant self-flattery of the English, nearly every Irishman is an anti-Irish Irishman. But here again popular phraseology hits the right word. This fairly educated and fairly wealthy Protestant wedge which is driven into the country at Dublin and elsewhere is a thing not easy superficially to summarise in any term. It cannot be described merely as a minority; for a minority means the part of a nation which is conquered. But this thing means something that conquers, and is not entirely part of a nation. Nor can one even fall back on the phrase of aristocracy. For an aristocracy implies at least some chorus of snobbish enthusiasm; it implies that some at least are willingly led by the leaders, if only towards vulgarity and vice. There is only one word for the minority in Ireland, and that is the word that public phraseology has found; I mean the word "Garrison." The Irish are essentially right when they talk as if all Protestant Unionists lived inside "The Castle." They have all the virtues and limitations of a literal garrison in a fort. That is, they are valiant, consistent, reliable in an obvious public sense; but their curse is that they can only tread the flagstones of the courtyard or the cold rock of the ramparts; they have never so much as set their foot upon their native soil.

We have considered Bernard Shaw as an Irishman. The next step is to consider him as an exile from Ireland living in Ireland; that, some people would say, is a paradox after his own heart. But, indeed, such a complication is not really difficult to expound. The great religion and the great national tradition which have persisted for so many centuries in Ireland have encouraged these clean and cutting elements; but they have encouraged many other things which serve to balance them. The Irish peasant has these qualities which are somewhat peculiar to Ireland, a strange purity and a strange pugnacity. But the Irish peasant also has qualities which are common to all peasants, and his nation has qualities that are common to all healthy nations. I mean chiefly the things that most of us absorb in childhood; especially the sense of the supernatural and the sense of the natural; the love of the sky with its infinity of vision, and the love of the soil with its strict hedges and solid shapes of ownership. But here comes the paradox of Shaw; the greatest of all his paradoxes and the one of which he is unconscious. These one or two plain truths which quite stupid people learn at the beginning are exactly the one or two truths which Bernard Shaw may not learn even at the end. He is a daring pilgrim who has set out from the grave to find the cradle. He started from points of view which no one else was clever enough to discover, and he is at last discovering points of view which no one else was ever stupid enough to ignore. This absence of the red-hot truisms of boyhood; this sense that he is not rooted in the ancient sagacities of infancy, has, I think, a great deal to do with his position as a member of an alien minority in Ireland. He who has no real country can have no real home. The average autochthonous Irishman is close to patriotism because he is close to the earth; he is close to domesticity because he is close to the earth; he is close to doctrinal theology and elaborate ritual because he is close to the earth. In short, he is close to the heavens because he is close to the earth. But we must not expect any of these elemental and collective virtues in the man of the garrison. He cannot be expected to exhibit the virtues of a people, but only (as Ibsen would say) of an enemy of the people. Mr. Shaw has no living traditions, no schoolboy tricks, no college customs, to link him with other men. Nothing about him can be supposed to refer to a family feud or to a family joke. He does not drink toasts; he does not keep anniversaries; musical as he is I doubt if he would consent to sing. All this has something in it of a tree with its roots in the air. The best way to shorten winter is to prolong Christmas; and the only way to enjoy the sun of April is to be an April Fool. When people asked Bernard Shaw to attend the Stratford Tercentenary, he wrote back with characteristic contempt: "I do not keep my own birthday, and I cannot see why I should keep Shakespeare's." I think that if Mr. Shaw had always kept his own birthday he would be better able to understand Shakespeare's birthday-- and Shakespeare's poetry.

In conjecturally referring this negative side of the man, his lack of the smaller charities of our common childhood, to his birth in the dominant Irish sect, I do not write without historic memory or reference to other cases. That minority of Protestant exiles which mainly represented Ireland to England during the eighteenth century did contain some specimens of the Irish lounger and even of the Irish blackguard; Sheridan and even Goldsmith suggest the type. Even in their irresponsibility these figures had a touch of Irish tartness and realism; but the type has been too much insisted on to the exclusion of others equally national and interesting. To one of these it is worth while to draw attention. At intervals during the eighteenth and nineteenth centuries there has appeared a peculiar kind of Irishman. He is so unlike the English image of Ireland that the English have actually fallen back on the pretence that he was not Irish at all. The type is commonly Protestant; and sometimes seems to be almost anti-national in its acrid instinct for judging itself. Its nationalism only appears when it flings itself with even bitterer pleasure into judging the foreigner or the invader. The first and greatest of such figures was Swift. Thackeray simply denied that Swift was an Irishman, because he was not a stage Irishman. He was not (in the English novelist's opinion) winning and agreeable enough to be Irish. The truth is that Swift was much too harsh and disagreeable to be English. There is a great deal of Jonathan Swift in Bernard Shaw. Shaw is like

Swift, for instance, in combining extravagant fancy with a curious sort of coldness. But he is most like Swift in that very quality which Thackeray said was impossible in an Irishman, benevolent bullying, a pity touched with contempt, and a habit of knocking men down for their own good. Characters in novels are often described as so amiable that they hate to be thanked. It is not an amiable quality, and it is an extremely rare one; but Swift possessed it. When Swift was buried the Dublin poor came in crowds and wept by the grave of the broadest and most freehanded of their benefactors. Swift deserved the public tribute; but he might have writhed and kicked in his grave at the thought of receiving it. There is in G. B. S. something of the same inhumane humanity. Irish history has offered a third instance of this particular type of educated and Protestant Irishman, sincere, unsympathetic, aggressive, alone. I mean Parnell; and with him also a bewildered England tried the desperate dodge of saying that he was not Irish at all. As if any thinkable sensible snobbish law-abiding Englishman would ever have defied all the drawing-rooms by disdaining the House of Commons! Despite the difference between taciturnity and a torrent of fluency there is much in common also between Shaw and Parnell; something in common even in the figures of the two men, in the bony bearded faces with their almost Satanic self-possession. It will not do to pretend that none of these three men belong to their own nation; but it is true that they belonged to one special, though recurring, type of that nation. And they all three have this peculiar mark, that while Nationalists in their various ways they all give to the more genial English one common impression; I mean the impression that they do not so much love Ireland as hate England.

I will not dogmatise upon the difficult question as to whether there is any religious significance in the fact that these three rather ruthless Irishmen were Protestant Irishmen. I incline to think myself that the Catholic Church has added charity and gentleness to the virtues of a people which would otherwise have been too keen and contemptuous, too aristocratic. But however this may be, there can surely be no question that Bernard Shaw's Protestant education in a Catholic country has made a great deal of difference to his mind. It has affected it in two ways, the first negative and the second positive. It has affected him by cutting him off (as we have said) from the fields and fountains of his real home and history; by making him an Orangeman. And it has affected him by the particular colour of the particular religion which he received; by making him a Puritan.

In one of his numerous prefaces he says, "I have always been on the side of the Puritans in the matter of Art"; and a closer study will, I think, reveal that he is on the side of the Puritans in almost everything. Puritanism was not a mere code of cruel regulations, though some of its regulations were more cruel than any that have disgraced Europe. Nor was Puritanism a mere nightmare, an evil shadow of eastern gloom and fatalism, though this element did enter it, and was as it were the symptom and punishment of its essential error. Something much nobler (even if almost equally mistaken) was the original energy in the Puritan creed. And it must be defined with a little more delicacy if we are really to understand the attitude of G. B. S., who is the greatest of the modern Puritans and perhaps the last.

I should roughly define the first spirit in Puritanism thus. It was a refusal to contemplate God or goodness with anything lighter or milder than the most fierce concentration of the intellect. A Puritan meant originally a man whose mind had no holidays. To use his own favourite phrase, he would let no living thing come between him and his God; an attitude which involved eternal torture for him and a cruel contempt for all the living things. It was better to worship in a barn than in a cathedral for the specific and specified reason that the cathedral was beautiful. Physical beauty was a false and sensual symbol coming in between the intellect and the object of its intellectual worship. The human brain ought to be at every instant a consuming fire which burns through all conventional images until they were as transparent as glass.

This is the essential Puritan idea, that God can only be praised by direct contemplation of Him. You must praise God only with your brain; it is wicked to praise Him with your passions or your physical habits or your gesture or instinct of beauty. Therefore it is wicked to worship by singing or dancing or drinking sacramental wines or building beautiful churches or saying prayers when you are half asleep. We must not worship by dancing, drinking, building or singing; we can only worship by thinking. Our heads can praise God, but never our hands and feet. That is the true and original impulse of the Puritans. There is a great deal to be said for it, and a great deal was said for it in Great Britain steadily for two hundred years. It has gradually decayed in England and Scotland, not because of the advance of modern thought (which means nothing), but because of the slow revival of the mediaeval energy and character in the two peoples. The English were always hearty and humane, and they have made up their minds to be hearty and humane in spite of the Puritans.

The result is that Dickens and W. W. Jacobs have picked up the tradition of Chaucer and Robin Hood. The Scotch were always romantic, and they have made up their minds to be romantic in spite of the Puritans. The result is that Scott and Stevenson have picked up the tradition of Bruce, Blind Harry and the vagabond Scottish kings. England has become English again; Scotland has become Scottish again, in spite of the splendid incubus, the noble nightmare of Calvin. There is only one place in the British Islands where one may naturally expect to find still surviving in its fulness the fierce detachment of the true Puritan. That place is the Protestant part of Ireland. The Orange Calvinists can be disturbed by no national resurrection, for they have no nation. In them, if in any people, will be found the rectangular consistency of the Calvinist. The Irish Protestant rioters are at least immeasurably finer fellows than any of their brethren in England. They have the two enormous superiorities: first, that the Irish Protestant rioters really believe in Protestant theology; and second, that the Irish Protestant rioters do really riot. Among these people, if anywhere, should be found the cult of theological clarity combined with barbarous external simplicity. Among these people Bernard Shaw was born.

There is at least one outstanding fact about the man we are studying; Bernard Shaw is never frivolous. He never gives his opinions a holiday; he is never irresponsible even for an instant. He has no nonsensical second self which he can get into as one gets into a dressing-gown; that ridiculous disguise which is yet more real than the real person. That collapse and humorous confession of futility was much of the force in Charles Lamb and in Stevenson. There is nothing of this in Shaw; his wit is never a weakness; therefore it is never a sense of humour. For wit is always connected with the idea that truth is close and clear. Humour, on the other hand, is always connected with the idea that truth is tricky and mystical and easily mistaken. What Charles Lamb said of the Scotchman is far truer of this type of Puritan Irishman; he does not see things suddenly in a new light; all his brilliancy is a blindingly rapid calculation and deduction. Bernard Shaw never said an indefensible thing; that is, he never said a thing that he was not prepared brilliantly to defend. He never breaks out into that cry beyond reason and conviction, that cry of Lamb when he cried, "We would indict our dreams!" or of Stevenson, "Shall we never shed blood?" In short he is not a humorist, but a great wit, almost as great as Voltaire. Humour is akin to agnosticism, which is only the negative side of mysticism. But pure wit is akin to Puritanism; to the perfect and painful consciousness of the final fact in the universe. Very briefly, the man who sees the consistency in things is a wit--and a Calvinist. The man who sees the inconsistency in things is a humorist--and a Catholic. However this may be, Bernard Shaw exhibits all that is purest in the Puritan; the desire to see truth face to face even if it slay us, the high impatience with irrelevant sentiment or obstructive symbol; the constant effort to keep the soul at its highest pressure and speed. His instincts upon all social customs and questions are Puritan. His favourite author is Bunyan.

But along with what was inspiring and direct in Puritanism Bernard Shaw has inherited also some of the things that were cumbersome and traditional. If ever Shaw exhibits a prejudice it is always a Puritan prejudice. For Puritanism has not been able to sustain through three centuries that native ecstasy of the direct contemplation of truth; indeed it was the whole mistake of Puritanism to imagine for a moment that it could. One cannot be serious for three hundred years. In institutions built so as to endure for ages you must have relaxation, symbolic relativity and healthy routine. In eternal temples you must have frivolity. You must "be at ease in Zion" unless you are only paying it a flying visit.

By the middle of the nineteenth century this old austerity and actuality in the Puritan vision had fallen away into two principal lower forms. The first is a sort of idealistic garrulity upon which Bernard Shaw has made fierce and on the whole fruitful war. Perpetual talk about righteousness and unselfishness, about things that should elevate and things which cannot but degrade, about social purity and true Christian manhood, all poured out with fatal fluency and with very little reference to the real facts of anybody's soul or salary--into this weak and lukewarm torrent has melted down much of that mountainous ice which sparkled in the seventeenth century, bleak indeed, but blazing. The hardest thing of the seventeenth century bids fair to be the softest thing of the twentieth.

Of all this sentimental and deliquescent Puritanism Bernard Shaw has always been the antagonist; and the only respect in which it has soiled him was that he believed for only too long that such sloppy idealism was the whole idealism of Christendom and so used "idealist" itself as a term of reproach. But there were other and negative effects of Puritanism which he did not escape so completely. I cannot think that he has wholly escaped that element in Puritanism which may fairly bear the title of the taboo. For it is a singular fact that although extreme Protestantism is dying in elaborate and over-refined civilisation, yet it is the barbaric patches of it that live longest and die last. Of the creed of John Knox the modern Protestant has abandoned the civilised part and retained only the savage part. He has given up that great and systematic philosophy of Calvinism which had much in common with modern science and strongly resembles ordinary and recurrent determinism. But he has retained the accidental veto upon cards or comic plays, which Knox only valued as mere proof of his people's concentration on their theology. All the awful but sublime affirmations of Puritan theology are gone. Only savage negations remain; such as that by which in Scotland on every seventh day the creed of fear lays his finger on all hearts and makes an evil silence in the streets.

By the middle of the nineteenth century when Shaw was born this dim and barbaric element in Puritanism, being all that remained of it, had added another taboo to its philosophy of taboos; there had grown up a mystical horror of those fermented drinks which are part of the food of civilised mankind. Doubtless many persons take an extreme line on this matter solely because of some calculation of social harm; many, but not all and not even most. Many people think that paper money is a mistake and does much harm. But they do not shudder or snigger when they see a cheque-book. They do not whisper with unsavoury slyness that such and such a man was "seen" going into a bank. I am quite convinced that the English aristocracy is the curse of England, but I have not noticed either in myself or others any disposition to ostracise a man simply for accepting a peerage, as the modern Puritans would certainly ostracise him (from any of their positions of trust) for accepting a drink. The sentiment is certainly very largely a mystical one, like the sentiment about the seventh day. Like the Sabbath, it is defended with sociological reasons; but those reasons can be simply and sharply tested. If a Puritan tells you that all humanity should rest once a week, you have only to propose that they should rest on Wednesday. And if a Puritan tells you that he does not object to beer but to the tragedies of excess in beer, simply propose to him that in prisons and workhouses (where the amount can be absolutely regulated) the inmates should have three glasses of beer a day. The Puritan cannot call that excess; but he will find something to call it. For it is not the excess he objects to, but the beer. It is a transcendental taboo, and it is one of the two or three positive and painful prejudices with which Bernard Shaw began. A similar severity of outlook ran through all his earlier attitude towards the drama; especially towards the lighter or looser drama. His Puritan teachers could not prevent him from taking up theatricals, but they made him take theatricals seriously. All his plays were indeed "plays for Puritans." All his criticisms quiver with a refined and almost tortured contempt for the indulgencies of ballet and burlesque, for the tights and the double entente. He can endure lawlessness but not levity. He is not repelled by the divorces and the adulteries as he is by the "splits." And he has always been foremost among the fierce modern critics who ask indignantly, "Why do you object to a thing full of sincere philosophy like The Wild Duck while you tolerate a mere dirty joke like The Spring Chicken?" I do not think he has ever understood what seems to me the very sensible answer of the man in the street, "I laugh at the dirty joke of The Spring Chicken because it is a joke. I criticise the philosophy of The Wild Duck because it is a philosophy."

Shaw does not do justice to the democratic ease and sanity on this subject; but indeed, whatever else he is, he is not democratic. As an Irishman he is an aristocrat, as a Calvinist he is a soul apart; he drew the breath of his nostrils from a land of fallen principalities and proud gentility, and the breath of his spirit from a creed which made a wall of crystal around the elect. The two forces between them produced this potent and slender figure, swift, scornful, dainty and full of dry magnanimity; and it only needed the last touch of oligarchic mastery to be given by the overwhelming oligarchic atmosphere of our present age. Such was the Puritan Irishman who stepped out into the world. Into what kind of world did he step?

* * * *

The Progressive

IT is now partly possible to justify the Shavian method of putting the explanations before the events. I can now give a fact or two with a partial certainty at least that the reader will give to the affairs of Bernard Shaw something of the same kind of significance which they have for Bernard Shaw himself. Thus, if I had simply said that Shaw was born in Dublin the average reader might exclaim, "Ah yes--a wild Irishman, gay, emotional and untrustworthy." The wrong note would be struck at the start. I have attempted to give some idea of what being born in Ireland meant to the man who was really born there. Now therefore for the first time I may be permitted to confess that Bernard Shaw was, like other men, born. He was born in Dublin on the 26th of July, 1856.

Just as his birth can only be appreciated through some vision of Ireland, so his family can only be appreciated by some realisation of the Puritan. He was the youngest son of one George Carr Shaw, who had been a civil servant and was afterwards a somewhat unsuccessful business man. If I had merely said that his family was Protestant (which in Ireland means Puritan) it might have been passed over as a quite colourless detail. But if the reader will keep in mind what has been said about the degeneration of Calvinism into a few clumsy vetoes, he will see in its full and frightful significance such a sentence as this which comes from Shaw himself: "My father was in theory a vehement teetotaller, but in practice often a furtive drinker." The two things of course rest upon exactly the same philosophy; the philosophy of the taboo. There is a mystical substance, and it can give monstrous pleasures or call down monstrous punishments. The dipsomaniac and the abstainer are not only both mistaken, but they both make the same mistake. They both regard wine as a drug and not as a drink. But if I had mentioned that fragment of family information without any ethical preface, people would have begun at once to talk nonsense about artistic heredity and Celtic weakness, and would have gained the general impression that Bernard Shaw was an Irish wastrel and the child of Irish wastrels. Whereas it is the whole point of the matter that Bernard Shaw comes of a Puritan middle-class family of the most solid respectability; and the only admission of error arises from the fact that one member of that Puritan family took a particularly Puritan view of strong drink. That is, he regarded it generally as a poison and sometimes as a medicine, if only a mental medicine. But a poison and a medicine are very closely akin, as the nearest chemist knows; and they are chiefly akin in this; that no one will drink either of them for fun. Moreover, medicine and a poison are also alike in this; that no one will by preference drink either of them in public. And this medical or poisonous view of alcohol is not confined to the one Puritan to whose failure I have referred, it is spread all over the whole of our dying Puritan civilisation. For instance, social reformers have fired a hundred shots against the public-house; but never one against its really shameful feature. The sign of decay is not in the public-house, but in the private bar; or rather the row of five or six private bars, into each of which a respectable dipsomaniac can go in solitude, and by indulging his own half-witted sin violate his own half-witted morality. Nearly all these places are equipped with an atrocious apparatus of ground-glass windows which can be so closed that they practically conceal the face of the buyer from the seller. Words cannot express the abysses of human infamy and hateful shame expressed by that elaborate piece of furniture. Whenever I go into a public-house, which happens fairly often, I always carefully open all these apertures and then leave the place, in every way refreshed.

In other ways also it is necessary to insist not only on the fact of an extreme Protestantism, but on that of the Protestantism of a garrison; a world where that religious force both grew and festered all the more for being at once isolated and protected. All the influences surrounding Bernard Shaw in boyhood were not only Puritan, but such that no non-Puritan force could possibly pierce or counteract. He belonged to that Irish group which, according to Catholicism, has hardened its heart, which, according to Protestantism has hardened its head, but which, as I fancy, has chiefly hardened its hide, lost its sensibility to the contact of the things around it. In reading about his youth, one forgets that it was passed in the island which is still one flame before the altar of St. Peter and St. Patrick. The whole thing might be happening in Wimbledon. He went to the Wesleyan Connexional School. He went to hear Moody and Sankey. "I was," he writes, "wholly unmoved by their eloquence; and felt bound to inform the public that I was, on the whole, an atheist. My letter was solemnly printed in Public Opinion, to the extreme horror of my numerous aunts and uncles." That is the philosophical atmosphere; those are the religious postulates. It could never cross the mind of a man of the Garrison that before becoming an atheist he might stroll into one of the churches of his own country, and learn something of the philosophy that had satisfied Dante and Bossuet, Pascal and Descartes.

In the same way I have to appeal to my theoretic preface at this third point of the drama of Shaw's career. On leaving school he stepped into a secure business position which he held steadily for four years and which he flung away almost in one day. He rushed even recklessly to London; where he was quite unsuccessful and practically starved for six years. If I had mentioned this act on the first page of this book it would have seemed to have either the simplicity of a mere fanatic or else to cover some ugly escapade of youth or some quite criminal looseness of temperament. But Bernard Shaw did not act thus because he was careless, but because he was ferociously careful, careful especially of the one thing needful. What was he thinking about when he threw away his last halfpence and went to a strange place; what was he thinking about when he endured hunger and small-pox in London almost without hope? He was thinking of what he has ever since thought of, the slow but sure surge of the social revolution; you must read into all those bald sentences and empty years what I shall attempt to sketch in the third section. You must read the revolutionary movement of the later nineteenth century, darkened indeed by materialism and made mutable by fear and free thought, but full of awful vistas of an escape from the curse of Adam.

Bernard Shaw happened to be born in an epoch, or rather at the end of an epoch, which was in its way unique in the ages of history. The nineteenth century was not unique in the success or rapidity of its reforms or in their ultimate cessation; but it was unique in the peculiar character of the failure which followed the success. The French Revolution was an enormous act of human realisation; it has altered the terms of every law and the shape of every town in Europe; but it was by no means the only example of a strong and swift period of reform. What was really peculiar about the Republican energy was this, that it left behind it, not an ordinary reaction but a kind of dreary, drawn out and utterly unmeaning hope. The strong and evident idea of reform sank lower and lower until it became the timid and feeble idea of progress. Towards the end of the nineteenth century there appeared its two incredible figures; they were the pure Conservative and the pure Progressive; two figures which would have been overwhelmed with laughter by any other intellectual commonwealth of history. There was hardly a human generation which could not have seen the folly of merely going forward or merely standing still; of mere progressing or mere conserving. In the coarsest Greek Comedy we might have a joke about a man who wanted to keep what he had, whether it was yellow gold or yellow fever. In the dullest mediaeval morality we might have a joke about a progressive gentleman who, having passed heaven and come to purgatory, decided to go further and fare worse. The twelfth and thirteenth centuries were an age of quite impetuous progress; men made in one rush, roads, trades, synthetic philosophies, parliaments, university settlements, a law that could cover the world and such spires as had never struck the sky. But they would not have said that they wanted progress, but that they wanted the road, the parliaments, and the spires. In the same way the time from Richelieu to the Revolution was upon the whole a time of conservation, often of harsh and hideous conservation; it preserved tortures, legal quibbles, and despotism. But if you had asked the rulers they would not have said that they wanted conservation; but that they wanted the torture and the despotism. The old reformers and the old despots alike desired definite things, powers, licenses, payments, vetoes, and permissions. Only the modern progressive and the modern conservative have been content with two words.

Other periods of active improvement have died by stiffening at last into some routine. Thus the Gothic gaiety of the thirteenth century stiffening into the mere Gothic ugliness of the fifteenth. Thus the mighty wave of the Renaissance, whose crest was lifted to heaven, was touched by a wintry witchery of classicism and frozen for ever before it fell. Alone of all such movements the democratic movement of the last two centuries has not frozen, but loosened and liquefied. Instead of becoming more pedantic in its old age, it has grown more bewildered. By the analogy of healthy history we ought to have gone on worshipping the republic and calling each other citizen, with increasing seriousness until some other part of the truth broke into our republican temple. But in fact we have turned the freedom of democracy into a mere scepticism, destructive of everything, including democracy itself. It is none the less destructive because it is, so to speak, an optimistic scepticism--or, as I have said, a dreary hope. It was none the better because the destroyers were always talking about the new vistas and enlightenments which their new negations opened to us. The republican temple, like any other strong building, rested on certain definite limits and supports. But the modern man inside it went on indefinitely knocking holes in his own house and saying that they were windows. The result is not hard to calculate: the moral world was pretty well all windows and no house by the time that Bernard Shaw arrived on the scene.

Then there entered into full swing that great game of which he soon became the greatest master. A progressive or advanced person was now to mean not a man who wanted democracy, but a man who wanted something newer than democracy. A reformer was to be, not a man who wanted a parliament or a republic, but a man who wanted anything that he hadn't got. The emancipated man must cast a weird and suspicious eye round him at all the institutions of the world, wondering which of them was destined to die in the next few centuries. Each one of them was whispering to himself, "What can I alter?"

This quite vague and varied discontent probably did lead to the revelation of many incidental wrongs and to much humane hard work in certain holes and corners. It also gave birth to a great deal of quite futile and frantic speculation, which seemed destined to take away babies from women, or to give votes to tom-cats. But it had an evil in it much deeper and more psychologically poisonous than any superficial absurdities. There was in this thirst to be "progressive" a subtle sort of double-mindedness and falsity. A man was so eager to be in advance of his age that he pretended to be in advance of himself. Institutions that his wholesome nature and habit fully accepted he had to sneer at as old-fashioned, out of a servile and snobbish fear of the future. Out of the primal forests, through all the real progress of history, man had picked his way obeying his human instinct, or (in the excellent phrase) following his nose. But now he was trying, by violent athletic exertions, to get in front of his nose.

Into this riot of all imaginary innovations Shaw brought the sharp edge of the Irishman and the concentration of the Puritan, and thoroughly thrashed all competitors in the difficult art of being at once modern and intelligent. In twenty twopenny controversies he took the revolutionary side, I fear in most cases because it was called revolutionary. But the other revolutionists were abruptly startled by the presentation of quite rational and ingenious arguments on their own side. The dreary thing about most new causes is that they are praised in such very old terms. Every new religion bores us with the same stale rhetoric about closer fellowship and the higher life. No one ever approximately equalled Bernard Shaw in the power of finding really fresh and personal arguments for these recent schemes and creeds. No one ever came within a mile of him in the knack of actually producing a new argument for a new philosophy. I give two instances to cover the kind of thing I mean. Bernard Shaw (being honestly eager to put himself on the modern side in everything) put himself on the side of what is called the feminist movement; the proposal to give the two sexes not merely equal social privileges, but identical. To this it is often answered that women cannot be soldiers; and to this again the sensible feminists answer that women run their own kind of physical risk, while the silly feminists answer that war is an outworn barbaric thing which women would abolish. But Bernard Shaw took the line of saying that women had been soldiers, in all occasions of natural and unofficial war, as in the French Revolution. That has the great fighting value of being an unexpected argument; it takes the other pugilist's breath away for one important instant. To take the other case, Mr. Shaw has found himself, led by the same mad imp of modernity, on the side of the people who want to have phonetic spelling. The people who want phonetic spelling generally depress the world with tireless and tasteless explanations of how much easier it would be for children or foreign bagmen if "height" were spelt "hite." Now children would curse spelling whatever it was, and we are not going to permit foreign bagmen to improve Shakespeare. Bernard Shaw charged along quite a different line; he urged that Shakespeare himself believed in phonetic spelling, since he spelt his own name in six different ways. According to Shaw, phonetic spelling is merely a return to the freedom and flexibility of Elizabethan literature. That, again, is exactly the kind of blow the old speller does not expect. As a matter of fact there is an answer to both the ingenuities I have quoted. When women have fought in revolutions they have generally shown that it was not natural to them, by their hysterical cruelty and insolence; it was the men who fought in the Revolution; it was the women who tortured the prisoners and mutilated the dead. And because Shakespeare could sing better than he could spell, it does not follow that his spelling and ours ought to be abruptly altered by a race that has lost all instinct for singing. But I do not wish to discuss these points; I only quote them as examples of the startling ability which really brought Shaw to the front; the ability to brighten even our modern movements with original and suggestive thoughts.

But while Bernard Shaw pleasantly surprised innumerable cranks and revolutionists by finding quite rational arguments for them, he surprised them unpleasantly also by discovering something else. He discovered a turn of argument or trick of thought which has ever since been the plague of their lives, and given him in all assemblies of their kind, in the Fabian Society or in the whole Socialist movement, a fantastic but most formidable domination. This method may be approximately defined as that of revolutionising the revolutionists by turning their rationalism against their remaining sentimentalism. But definition leaves the matter dark unless we give one or two examples. Thus Bernard Shaw threw himself as thoroughly as any New Woman into the cause of the emancipation of women. But while the New Woman praised woman as a prophetess, the new man took the opportunity to curse her and kick her as a comrade. For the others sex equality meant the emancipation of women, which allowed them to be equal to men. For Shaw it mainly meant the emancipation of men, which allowed them to be rude to women. Indeed, almost every one of Bernard Shaw's earlier plays might be called an argument between a man and a woman, in which the woman is thumped and thrashed and outwitted until she admits that she is the equal of her conqueror. This is the first case of the Shavian trick of turning on the romantic rationalists with their own rationalism. He said in substance, "If we are democrats, let us have votes for women; but if we are democrats, why on earth should we have respect for women?" I take one other example out of many. Bernard Shaw was thrown early into what may be called the cosmopolitan club of revolution. The Socialists of the S. D. F. call it "L'Internationale," but the club covers more than Socialists. It covers many who consider themselves the champions of oppressed nationalities-- Poland, Finland, and even Ireland; and thus a strong nationalist tendency exists in the revolutionary movement. Against this nationalist tendency Shaw set himself with sudden violence. If the flag of England was a piece of piratical humbug, was not the flag of Poland a piece of piratical humbug too? If we hated the jingoism of the existing armies and frontiers, why should we bring into existence new jingo armies and new jingo frontiers? All the other revolutionists fell in instinctively with Home Rule for Ireland. Shaw urged, in effect, that Home Rule was as bad as Home Influences and Home Cooking, and all the other degrading domesticities that began with the word "Home." His ultimate support of the South African war was largely created by his irritation against the other revolutionists for favouring a nationalist resistance. The ordinary Imperialists objected to Pro-Boers because they were anti-patriots. Bernard Shaw objected to Pro-Boers because they were pro-patriots.

But among these surprise attacks of G. B. S., these turnings of scepticism against the sceptics, there was one which has figured largely in his life; the most amusing and perhaps the most salutary of all these reactions. The "progressive" world being in revolt against religion had naturally felt itself allied to science; and against the authority of priests it would perpetually hurl the authority of scientific men. Shaw gazed for a few moments at this new authority, the veiled god of Huxley and Tyndall, and then with the greatest placidity and precision kicked it in the stomach. He declared to the astounded progressives around him that physical science was a mystical fake like sacerdotalism; that scientists, like priests, spoke with authority because they could not speak with proof or reason; that the very wonders of science were mostly lies, like the wonders of religion. "When astronomers tell me", he says somewhere, "that a star is so far off that its light takes a thousand years to reach us, the magnitude of the lie seems to me inartistic." The paralysing impudence of such remarks left everyone quite breathless; and even to this day this particular part of Shaw's satiric war has been far less followed up than it deserves. For there was present in it an element very marked in Shaw's controversies; I mean that his apparent exaggerations are generally much better backed up by knowledge than would appear from their nature. He can lure his enemy on with fantasies and then overwhelm him with facts. Thus the man of science, when he read some wild passage in which Shaw compared Huxley to a tribal soothsayer grubbing in the entrails of animals, supposed the writer to be a mere fantastic whom science could crush with one finger. He would therefore engage in a controversy with Shaw about (let us say) vivisection, and discover to his horror that Shaw really knew a great deal about the subject, and could pelt him with expert witnesses and hospital reports. Among the many singular contradictions in a singular character, there is none more interesting than this combination of exactitude and industry in the detail of opinions with audacity and a certain wildness in their outline.

This great game of catching revolutionists napping, of catching the unconventional people in conventional poses, of outmarching and outmanoeuvring progressives till they felt like conservatives, of undermining the mines of Nihilists till they felt like the House of Lords, this great game of dishing the anarchists continued for some time to be his most effective business. It would be untrue to say that he was a cynic; he was never a cynic, for that implies a certain corrupt fatigue about human affairs, whereas he was vibrating with virtue and energy. Nor would it be fair to call him even a sceptic, for that implies a dogma of hopelessness and definite belief in unbelief. But it would be strictly just to describe him at this time, at any rate, as a merely destructive person. He was one whose main business was, in his own view, the pricking of illusions, the stripping away of disguises, and even the destruction of ideals. He was a sort of anti-confectioner whose whole business it was to take the gilt off the gingerbread.

Now I have no particular objection to people who take the gilt off the gingerbread; if only for this excellent reason, that I am much fonder of gingerbread than I am of gilt. But there are some objections to this task when it becomes a crusade or an obsession. One of them is this: that people who have really scraped the gilt off gingerbread generally waste the rest of their lives in attempting to scrape the gilt off gigantic lumps of gold. Such has too often been the case of Shaw. He can, if he likes, scrape the romance off the armaments of Europe or the party system of Great Britain. But he cannot scrape the romance off love or military valour, because it is all romance, and three thousand miles thick. It cannot, I think, be denied that much of Bernard Shaw's splendid mental energy has been wasted in this weary business of gnawing at the necessary pillars of all possible society. But it would be grossly unfair to indicate that even in his first and most destructive stage he uttered nothing except these accidental, if arresting, negations. He threw his whole genius heavily into the scale in favour of two positive projects or causes of the period. When we have stated these we have really stated the full intellectual equipment with which he started his literary life.

I have said that Shaw was on the insurgent side in everything; but in the case of these two important convictions he exercised a solid power of choice. When he first went to London he mixed with every kind of revolutionary society, and met every kind of person except the ordinary person. He knew everybody, so to speak, except everybody. He was more than once a momentary apparition among the respectable atheists. He knew Bradlaugh and spoke on the platforms of that Hall of Science in which very simple and sincere masses of men used to hail with shouts of joy the assurance that they were not immortal. He retains to this day something of the noise and narrowness of that room; as, for instance, when he says that it is contemptible to have a craving for eternal life. This prejudice remains in direct opposition to all his present opinions, which are all to the effect that it is glorious to desire power, consciousness, and vitality even for one's self. But this old secularist tag, that it is selfish to save one's soul, remains with him long after he has practically glorified selfishness. It is a relic of those chaotic early days. And just as he mingled with the atheists he mingled with the anarchists, who were in the eighties a much more formidable body than now, disputing with the Socialists on almost equal terms the claim to be the true heirs of the Revolution. Shaw still talks entertainingly about this group. As far as I can make out, it was almost entirely female. When a book came out called A Girl among the Anarchists, G. B. S. was provoked to a sort of explosive reminiscence. "A girl among the anarchists!" he exclaimed to his present biographer; "if they had said 'A man among the anarchists' it would have been more of an adventure." He is ready to tell other tales of this eccentric environment, most of which does not convey an impression of a very bracing atmosphere. That revolutionary society must have contained many high public ideals, but also a fair number of low private desires. And when people blame Bernard Shaw for his pitiless and prosaic coldness, his cutting refusal to reverence or admire, I think they should remember this riff-raff of lawless sentimentalism against which his common-sense had to strive, all the grandiloquent "comrades" and all the gushing "affinities," all the sweetstuff sensuality and senseless sulking against law. If

Bernard Shaw became a little too fond of throwing cold water upon prophecies or ideals, remember that he must have passed much of his youth among cosmopolitan idealists who wanted a little cold water in every sense of the word.

Upon two of these modern crusades he concentrated, and, as I have said, he chose them well. The first was broadly what was called the Humanitarian cause. It did not mean the cause of humanity, but rather, if anything, the cause of everything else. At its noblest it meant a sort of mystical identification of our life with the whole life of nature. So a man might wince when a snail was crushed as if his toe were trodden on; so a man might shrink when a moth shrivelled as if his own hair had caught fire. Man might be a network of exquisite nerves running over the whole universe, a subtle spider's web of pity. This was a fine conception; though perhaps a somewhat severe enforcement of the theological conception of the special divinity of man. For the humanitarians certainly asked of humanity what can be asked of no other creature; no man ever required a dog to understand a cat or expected the cow to cry for the sorrows of the nightingale.

Hence this sense has been strongest in saints of a very mystical sort; such as St. Francis who spoke of Sister Sparrow and Brother Wolf. Shaw adopted this crusade of cosmic pity but adopted it very much in his own style, severe, explanatory, and even unsympathetic. He had no affectionate impulse to say "Brother Wolf"; at the best he would have said "Citizen Wolf," like a sound republican. In fact, he was full of healthy human compassion for the sufferings of animals; but in phraseology he loved to put the matter unemotionally and even harshly. I was once at a debating club at which Bernard Shaw said that he was not a humanitarian at all, but only an economist, that he merely hated to see life wasted by carelessness or cruelty. I felt inclined to get up and address to him the following lucid question: "If when you spare a herring you are only being oikonomikal, for what oikos are you being nomikal?" But in an average debating club I thought this question might not be quite clear; so I abandoned the idea. But certainly it is not plain for whom Bernard Shaw is economising if he rescues a rhinoceros from an early grave. But the truth is that Shaw only took this economic pose from his hatred of appearing sentimental. If Bernard Shaw killed a dragon and rescued a princess of romance, he would try to say "I have saved a princess" with exactly the same intonation as "I have saved a shilling." He tries to turn his own heroism into a sort of superhuman thrift. He would thoroughly sympathise with that passage in his favourite dramatic author in which the Button Moulder tells Peer Gynt that there is a sort of cosmic housekeeping; that God Himself is very economical, "and that is why He is so well to do."

This combination of the widest kindness and consideration with a consistent ungraciousness of tone runs through all Shaw's ethical utterance, and is nowhere more evident than in his attitude towards animals. He would waste himself to a white-haired shadow to save a shark in an aquarium from inconvenience or to add any little comforts to the life of a carrion-crow. He would defy any laws or lose any friends to show mercy to the humblest beast or the most hidden bird. Yet I cannot recall in the whole of his works or in the whole of his conversation a single word of any tenderness or intimacy with any bird or beast. It was under the influence of this high and almost superhuman sense of duty that he became a vegetarian; and I seem to remember that when he was lying sick and near to death at the end of his Saturday Review career he wrote a fine fantastic article, declaring that his hearse ought to be drawn by all the animals that he had not eaten. Whenever that evil day comes there will be no need to fall back on the ranks of the brute creation; there will be no lack of men and women who owe him so much as to be glad to take the place of the animals; and the present writer for one will be glad to express his gratitude as an elephant. There is no doubt about the essential manhood and decency of Bernard Shaw's instincts in such matters. And quite apart from the vegetarian controversy, I do not doubt that the beasts also owe him much. But when we come to positive things (and passions are the only truly positive things) that obstinate doubt remains which remains after all eulogies of Shaw. That fixed fancy sticks to the mind; that Bernard Shaw is a vegetarian more because he dislikes dead beasts than because he likes live ones.

It was the same with the other great cause to which Shaw more politically though not more publicly committed himself. The actual English people, without representation in Press or Parliament, but faintly expressed in public-houses and music-halls, would connect Shaw (so far as they have heard of him) with two ideas; they would say first that he was a vegetarian, and second that he was a Socialist. Like most of the impressions of the ignorant, these impressions would be on the whole very just. My only purpose here is to urge that Shaw's Socialism exemplifies the same trait of temperament as his vegetarianism. This book is not concerned with Bernard Shaw as a politician or a sociologist, but as a critic and creator of drama. I will therefore end in this chapter all that I have to say about Bernard Shaw as a politician or a political philosopher. I propose here to dismiss this aspect of Shaw: only let it be remembered, once and for all, that I am here dismissing the most important aspect of Shaw. It is as if one dismissed the sculpture of Michael Angelo and went on to his sonnets. Perhaps the highest and purest thing in him is simply that he cares more for politics than for anything else; more than for art or for philosophy. Socialism is the noblest thing for Bernard Shaw; and it is the noblest thing in him. He really desires less to win fame than to bear fruit. He is an absolute follower of that early sage who wished only to make two blades of grass grow instead of one. He is a loyal subject of Henri Quatre, who said that he only wanted every Frenchman to have a chicken in his pot on Sunday; except, of course, that he would call the repast cannibalism. But caeteris paribus he thinks more of that chicken than of the eagle of the universal empire; and he is always ready to support the grass against the laurel.

Yet by the nature of this book the account of the most important Shaw, who is the Socialist, must be also the most brief. Socialism (which I am not here concerned either to attack or defend) is, as everyone knows, the proposal that all property should be nationally owned that it may be more decently distributed. It is a proposal resting upon two principles, unimpeachable as far as they go: first, that frightful human calamities call for immediate human aid; second, that such aid must almost always be collectively organised. If a ship is being wrecked, we organise a lifeboat; if a house is on fire, we organise a blanket; if half a nation is starving, we must organise work and food. That is the primary and powerful argument of the Socialist, and everything that he adds to it weakens it. The only possible line of protest is to suggest that it is rather shocking that we have to treat a normal nation as something exceptional, like a house on fire or a shipwreck. But of such things it may be necessary to speak later. The point here is that Shaw behaved towards Socialism just as he behaved towards vegetarianism; he offered every reason except the emotional reason, which was the real one. When taxed in a Daily News discussion with being a Socialist for the obvious reason that poverty was cruel, he said this was quite wrong; it was only because poverty was wasteful. He practically professed that modern society annoyed him, not so much like an unrighteous kingdom, but rather like an untidy room. Everyone who knew him knew, of course, that he was full of a proper brotherly bitterness about the oppression of the poor. But here again he would not admit that he was anything but an Economist.

In thus setting his face like flint against sentimental methods of argument he undoubtedly did one great service to the causes for which he stood. Every vulgar anti-humanitarian, every snob who wants monkeys vivisected or beggars flogged has always fallen back upon stereotyped phrases like "maudlin" and "sentimental," which indicated the humanitarian as a man in a weak condition of tears. The mere personality of Shaw has shattered those foolish phrases for ever. Shaw the humanitarian was like Voltaire the humanitarian, a man whose satire was like steel, the hardest and coolest of fighters, upon whose piercing point the wretched defenders of a masculine brutality wriggled like worms.

In this quarrel one cannot wish Shaw even an inch less contemptuous, for the people who call compassion "sentimentalism" deserve nothing but contempt. In this one does not even regret his coldness; it is an honourable contrast to the blundering emotionalism of the jingoes and flagellomaniacs. The truth is that the ordinary anti-humanitarian only manages to harden his heart by having already softened his head. It is the reverse of sentimental to insist that a nigger is being burned alive; for sentimentalism must be the clinging to pleasant thoughts. And no one, not even a Higher Evolutionist, can think a nigger burned alive a pleasant thought. The sentimental thing is to warm your hands at the fire while denying the existence of the nigger, and that is the ruling habit in England, as it has been the chief business of Bernard Shaw to show. And in this the brutalitarians hate him not because he is soft, but because he is hard, because he is not to be softened by conventional excuses; because he looks hard at a thing--and hits harder. Some foolish fellow of the Henley-Whibley reaction wrote that if we were to be conquerors we must be less tender and more ruthless. Shaw answered with really avenging irony, "What a light this principle throws on the defeat of the tender Dervish, the compassionate Zulu, and the morbidly humane Boxer at the hands of the hardy savages of England, France, and Germany." In that sentence an idiot is obliterated and the whole story of Europe told; but it is immensely stiffened by its ironic form. In the same way Shaw washed away for ever the idea that Socialists were weak dreamers, who said that things might be only because they wished them to be. G. B. S. in argument with an individualist showed himself, as a rule, much the better economist and much the worse rhetorician. In this atmosphere arose a celebrated Fabian Society, of which he is still the leading spirit--a society which answered all charges of impracticable idealism by pushing both its theoretic statements and its practical negotiations to the verge of cynicism. Bernard Shaw was the literary expert who wrote most of its pamphlets. In one of them, among such sections as _Fabian Temperance Reform, Fabian Education_ and so on, there was an entry gravely headed "Fabian Natural Science," which stated that in the Socialist cause light was needed more than heat.

Thus the Irish detachment and the Puritan austerity did much good to the country and to the causes for which they were embattled. But there was one thing they did not do; they did nothing for Shaw himself in the matter of his primary mistakes and his real limitation. His great defect was and is the lack of democratic sentiment. And there was nothing democratic either in his humanitarianism or his Socialism. These new and refined faiths tended rather to make the Irishman yet more aristocratic, the Puritan yet more exclusive. To be a Socialist was to look down on all the peasant owners of the earth, especially on the peasant owners of his own island. To be a Vegetarian was to be a man with a strange and mysterious morality, a man who thought the good lord who roasted oxen for his vassals only less bad than the bad lord who roasted the vassals. None of these advanced views could the common people hear gladly; nor indeed was Shaw specially anxious to please the common people. It was his glory that he pitied animals like men; it was his defect that he pitied men only too much like animals. Foulon said of the democracy, "Let them eat grass." Shaw said, "Let them eat greens." He had more benevolence, but almost as much disdain. "I have never had any feelings about the English working classes," he said elsewhere, "except a desire to abolish them and replace them by sensible people." This is the unsympathetic side of the thing; but it had another and much nobler side, which must at least be seriously recognised before we pass on to much lighter things.

Bernard Shaw is not a democrat; but he is a splendid republican. The nuance of difference between those terms precisely depicts him. And there is after all a good deal of dim democracy in England, in the sense that there is much of a blind sense of brotherhood, and nowhere more than among old-fashioned and even reactionary people. But a republican is a rare bird, and a noble one. Shaw is a republican in the literal and Latin sense; he cares more for the Public Thing than for any private thing. The interest of the State is with him a sincere thirst of the soul, as it was in the little pagan cities. Now this public passion, this clean appetite for order and equity, had fallen to a lower ebb, had more nearly disappeared altogether, during Shaw's earlier epoch than at any other time. Individualism of the worst type was on the top of the wave; I mean artistic individualism, which is so much crueller, so much blinder and so much more irrational even than commercial individualism. The decay of society was praised by artists as the decay of a corpse is praised by worms. The aesthete was all receptiveness, like the flea. His only affair in this world was to feed on its facts and colours, like a parasite upon blood. The ego was the all; and the praise of it was enunciated in madder and madder rhythms by poets whose Helicon was absinthe and whose Pegasus was the nightmare. This diseased pride was not even conscious of a public interest, and would have found all political terms utterly tasteless and insignificant. It was no longer a question of one man one vote, but of one man one universe.

I have in my time had my fling at the Fabian Society, at the pedantry of schemes, the arrogance of experts; nor do I regret it now. But when I remember that other world against which it reared its bourgeois banner of cleanliness and common sense, I will not end this chapter without doing it decent honour. Give me the drain pipes of the Fabians rather than the panpipes of the later poets; the drain pipes have a nicer smell. Give me even that businesslike benevolence that herded men like beasts rather than that exquisite art which isolated them like devils; give me even the suppression of "Zaeo" rather than the triumph of "Salome." And if I feel such a confession to be due to those Fabians who could hardly have been anything but experts in any society, such as Mr. Sidney Webb or Mr. Edward Pease, it is due yet more strongly to the greatest of the Fabians. Here was a man who could have enjoyed art among the artists, who could have been the wittiest of all the fl 鈔 eurs; who could have made epigrams like diamonds and drunk music like wine. He has instead laboured in a mill of statistics and crammed his mind with all the most dreary and the most filthy details, so that he can argue on the spur of the moment about sewing-machines or sewage, about typhus fever or twopenny tubes. The usual mean theory of motives will not cover the case; it is not ambition, for he could have been twenty times more prominent as a plausible and popular humorist. It is the real and ancient emotion of the salus populi, almost extinct in our oligarchical chaos; nor will I for one, as I pass on to many matters of argument or quarrel, neglect to salute a passion so implacable and so pure.

* * * *

The Critic

IT appears a point of some mystery to the present writer that Bernard Shaw should have been so long unrecognised and almost in beggary. I should have thought his talent was of the ringing and arresting sort; such as even editors and publishers would have sense enough to seize. Yet it is quite certain that he almost starved in London for many years, writing occasional columns for an advertisement or words for a picture. And it is equally certain (it is proved by twenty anecdotes, but no one who knows Shaw needs any anecdotes to prove it) that in those days of desperation he again and again threw up chances and flung back good bargains which did not suit his unique and erratic sense of honour. The fame of having first offered Shaw to the public upon a platform worthy of him belongs, like many other public services, to Mr. William Archer.

I say it seems odd that such a writer should not be appreciated in a flash; but upon this point there is evidently a real difference of opinion, and it constitutes for me the strangest difficulty of the subject. I hear many people complain that Bernard Shaw deliberately mystifies them. I cannot imagine what they mean; it seems to me that he deliberately insults them. His language, especially on moral questions, is generally as straight and solid as that of a bargee and far less ornate and symbolic than that of a hansom-cabman. The prosperous English Philistine complains that Mr. Shaw is making a fool of him. Whereas Mr. Shaw is not in the least making a fool of him; Mr. Shaw is, with laborious lucidity, calling him a fool. G. B. S. calls a landlord a thief; and the landlord, instead of denying or resenting it, says, "Ah, that fellow hides his meaning so cleverly that one can never make out what he means, it is all so fine spun and fantastical." G. B. S. calls a statesman a liar to his face, and the statesman cries in a kind of ecstasy, "Ah, what quaint, intricate and half-tangled trains of thought! Ah, what elusive and many-coloured mysteries of half-meaning!" I think it is always quite plain what Mr. Shaw means, even when he is joking, and it generally means that the people he is talking to ought to howl aloud for their sins. But the average representative of them undoubtedly treats the Shavian meaning as tricky and complex, when it is really direct and offensive. He always accuses Shaw of pulling his leg, at the exact moment when Shaw is pulling his nose.

This prompt and pungent style he learnt in the open, upon political tubs and platforms; and he is very legitimately proud of it. He boasts of being a demagogue; "The cart and the trumpet for me," he says, with admirable good sense. Everyone will remember the effective appearance of Cyrano de Bergerac in the first act of the fine play of that name; when instead of leaping in by any hackneyed door or window, he suddenly springs upon a chair above the crowd that has so far kept him invisible; "les bras crois 閱, le feutre en bataille, la moustache heriss 閑, le nez terrible." I will not go so far as to say that when Bernard Shaw sprang upon a chair or tub in Trafalgar Square he had the hat in battle, or even that he had the nose terrible. But just as we see Cyrano best when he thus leaps above the crowd, I think we may take this moment of Shaw stepping on his little platform to see him clearly as he then was, and even as he has largely not ceased to be. I, at least, have only known him in his middle age; yet I think I can see him, younger yet only a little more alert, with hair more red but with face yet paler, as he first stood up upon some cart or barrow in the tossing glare of the gas.

The first fact that one realises about Shaw (independent of all one has read and often contradicting it) is his voice. Primarily it is the voice of an Irishman, and then something of the voice of a musician. It possibly explains much of his career; a man may be permitted to say so many impudent things with so pleasant an intonation. But the voice is not only Irish and agreeable, it is also frank and as it were inviting conference. This goes with a style and gesture which can only be described as at once very casual and very emphatic. He assumes that bodily supremacy which goes with oratory, but he assumes it with almost ostentatious carelessness; he throws back the head, but loosely and laughingly. He is at once swaggering and yet shrugging his shoulders, as if to drop from them the mantle of the orator which he has confidently assumed. Lastly, no man ever used voice or gesture better for the purpose of expressing certainty; no man can say "I tell Mr. Jones he is totally wrong" with more air of unforced and even casual conviction.

This particular play of feature or pitch of voice, at once didactic and yet not uncomrade-like, must be counted a very important fact, especially in connection with the period when that voice was first heard. It must be remembered that Shaw emerged as a wit in a sort of secondary age of wits; one of those stale interludes of prematurely old young men, which separate the serious epochs of history. Oscar Wilde was its god; but he was somewhat more mystical, not to say monstrous, than the average of its dried and decorous impudence. The two survivals of that time, as far as I know, are Mr. Max Beerbohm and Mr. Graham Robertson; two most charming people; but the air they had to live in was the devil. One of its notes was an artificial reticence of speech, which waited till it could plant the perfect epigram. Its typical products were far too conceited to lay down the law. Now when people heard that Bernard Shaw was witty, as he most certainly was, when they heard his mots repeated like those of Whistler or Wilde, when they heard things like "the Seven deadly Virtues" or "Who was Hall Caine?" they expected another of these silent sarcastic dandies who went about with one epigram, patient and poisonous, like a bee with his one sting. And when they saw and heard the new humorist they found no fixed sneer, no frock coat, no green carnation, no silent Savoy Restaurant good manners, no fear of looking a fool, no particular notion of looking a gentleman. They found a talkative Irishman with a kind voice and a brown coat; open gestures and an evident desire to make people really agree with him. He had his own kind of affectations no doubt, and his own kind of tricks of debate; but he broke, and, thank God, forever the spell of the little man with the single eye glass who had frozen both faith and fun at so many tea-tables. Shaw's humane voice and hearty manner were so obviously more the things of a great man than the hard, gem-like brilliancy of Wilde or the careful ill-temper of Whistler. He brought in a breezier sort of insolence; the single eye-glass fled before the single eye.

Added to the effect of the amiable dogmatic voice and lean, loose swaggering figure, is that of the face with which so many caricaturists have fantastically delighted themselves, the Mephistophilean face with the fierce tufted eyebrows and forked red beard. Yet those caricaturists in their natural delight in coming upon so striking a face, have somewhat misrepresented it, making it merely Satanic; whereas its actual expression has quite as much benevolence as mockery. By this time his costume has become a part of his personality; one has come to think of the reddish brown Jaeger suit as if it were a sort of reddish brown fur, and were, like the hair and eyebrows, a part of the animal; yet there are those who claim to remember a Bernard Shaw of yet more awful aspect before Jaeger came to his assistance; a Bernard Shaw in a dilapidated frock-coat and some sort of straw hat. I can hardly believe it; the man is so much of a piece, and must always have dressed appropriately. In any case his brown woollen clothes, at once artistic and hygienic, completed the appeal for which he stood; which might be defined as an eccentric healthy-mindedness. But something of the vagueness and equivocation of his first fame is probably due to the different functions which he performed in the contemporary world of art.

He began by writing novels. They are not much read, and indeed not imperatively worth reading, with the one exception of the crude and magnificent Cashel Byron's Profession. Mr. William Archer, in the course of his kindly efforts on behalf of his young Irish friend, sent this book to Samoa, for the opinion of the most elvish and yet efficient of modern critics. Stevenson summed up much of Shaw even from that fragment when he spoke of a romantic griffin roaring with laughter at the nature of his own quest. He also added the not wholly unjustified post-script: "I say, Archer,-- my God, what women!"

The fiction was largely dropped; but when he began work he felt his way by the avenues of three arts. He was an art critic, a dramatic critic, and a musical critic; and in all three, it need hardly be said, he fought for the newest style and the most revolutionary school. He wrote on all these as he would have written on anything; but it was, I fancy, about the music that he cared most.

It may often be remarked that mathematicians love and understand music more than they love or understand poetry. Bernard Shaw is in much the same condition; indeed, in attempting to do justice to Shakespeare's poetry, he always calls it "word music." It is not difficult to explain this special attachment of the mere logician to music. The logician, like every other man on earth, must have sentiment and romance in his existence; in every man's life, indeed, which can be called a life at all, sentiment is the most solid thing. But if the extreme logician turns for his emotions to poetry, he is exasperated and bewildered by discovering that the words of his own trade are used in an entirely different meaning. He conceives that he understands the word "visible," and then finds Milton applying it to darkness, in which nothing is visible. He supposes that he understands the word "hide," and then finds Shelley talking of a poet hidden in the light. He has reason to believe that he understands the common word "hung"; and then William Shakespeare, Esquire, of Stratford-on-Avon, gravely assures him that the tops of the tall sea waves were hung with deafening clamours on the slippery clouds. That is why the common arithmetician prefers music to poetry. Words are his scientific instruments. It irritates him that they should be anyone else's musical instruments. He is willing to see men juggling, but not men juggling with his own private tools and possessions-- his terms. It is then that he turns with an utter relief to music. Here are all the same fascination and inspiration, all the same purity and plunging force as in poetry; but not requiring any verbal confession that light conceals things or that darkness can be seen in the dark. Music is mere beauty; it is beauty in the abstract, beauty in solution. It is a shapeless and liquid element of beauty, in which a man may really float, not indeed affirming the truth, but not denying it. Bernard Shaw, as I have already said, is infinitely far above all such mere mathematicians and pedantic reasoners; still his feeling is partly the same. He adores music because it cannot deal with romantic terms either in their right or their wrong sense. Music can be romantic without reminding him of Shakespeare and Walter Scott, with whom he has had personal, quarrels. Music can be Catholic without reminding him verbally of the Catholic Church, which he has never seen, and is sure he does not like. Bernard Shaw can agree with Wagner, the musician, because he speaks without words; if it had been Wagner the man he would certainly have had words with him. Therefore I would suggest that Shaw's love of music (which is so fundamental that it must be mentioned early, if not first, in his story) may itself be considered in the first case as the imaginative safety-valve of the rationalistic Irishman.

This much may be said conjecturally over the present signature; but more must not be said. Bernard Shaw understands music so much better than I do that it is just possible that he is, in that tongue and atmosphere, all that he is not elsewhere. While he is writing with a pen I know his limitations as much as I admire his genius; and I know it is true to say that he does not appreciate romance. But while he is playing on the piano he may be cocking a feather, drawing a sword or draining a flagon for all I know. While he is speaking I am sure that there are some things he does not understand. But while he is listening (at the Queen's Hall) he may understand everything, including God and me. Upon this part of him I am a reverent agnostic; it is well to have some such dark continent in the character of a man of whom one writes. It preserves two very important things--modesty in the biographer and mystery in the biography.

For the purpose of our present generalisation it is only necessary to say that Shaw, as a musical critic, summed himself up as "The Perfect Wagnerite"; he threw himself into subtle and yet trenchant eulogy of that revolutionary voice in music. It was the same with the other arts. As he was a Perfect Wagnerite in music, so he was a Perfect Whistlerite in painting; so above all he was a Perfect Ibsenite in drama. And with this we enter that part of his career with which this book is more specially concerned. When Mr. William Archer got him established as dramatic critic of the Saturday Review, he became for the first time "a star of the stage"; a shooting star and sometimes a destroying comet.

On the day of that appointment opened one of the very few exhilarating and honest battles that broke the silence of the slow and cynical collapse of the nineteenth century. Bernard Shaw the demagogue had got his cart and his trumpet; and was resolved to make them like the car of destiny and the trumpet of judgment. He had not the servility of the ordinary rebel, who is content to go on rebelling against kings and priests, because such rebellion is as old and as established as any priests or kings. He cast about him for something to attack which was not merely powerful or placid, but was unattacked. After a little quite sincere reflection, he found it. He would not be content to be a common atheist; he wished to blaspheme something in which even atheists believed. He was not satisfied with being revolutionary; there were so many revolutionists. He wanted to pick out some prominent institution which had been irrationally and instinctively accepted by the most violent and profane; something of which Mr. Foote would speak as respectfully on the front page of the Freethinker as Mr. St. Loe Strachey on the front page of the Spectator. He found the thing; he found the great unassailed English institution--Shakespeare.

But Shaw's attack on Shakespeare, though exaggerated for the fun of the thing, was not by any means the mere folly or firework paradox that has been supposed. He meant what he said; what was called his levity was merely the laughter of a man who enjoyed saying what he meant-- an occupation which is indeed one of the greatest larks in life. Moreover, it can honestly be said that Shaw did good by shaking the mere idolatry of Him of Avon. That idolatry was bad for England; it buttressed our perilous self-complacency by making us think that we alone had, not merely a great poet, but the one poet above criticism. It was bad for literature; it made a minute model out of work that was really a hasty and faulty masterpiece. And it was bad for religion and morals that there should be so huge a terrestrial idol, that we should put such utter and unreasoning trust in any child of man. It is true that it was largely through Shaw's own defects that he beheld the defects of Shakespeare. But it needed someone equally prosaic to resist what was perilous in the charm of such poetry; it may not be altogether a mistake to send a deaf man to destroy the rock of the sirens.

This attitude of Shaw illustrates of course all three of the divisions or aspects to which the reader's attention has been drawn. It was partly the attitude of the Irishman objecting to the Englishman turning his mere artistic taste into a religion; especially when it was a taste merely taught him by his aunts and uncles. In Shaw's opinion (one might say) the English do not really enjoy Shakespeare or even admire Shakespeare; one can only say, in the strong colloquialism, that they swear by Shakespeare. He is a mere god; a thing to be invoked. And Shaw's whole business was to set up the things which were to be sworn by as things to be sworn at. It was partly again the revolutionist in pursuit of pure novelty, hating primarily the oppression of the past, almost hating history itself. For Bernard Shaw the prophets were to be stoned after, and not before, men had built their sepulchres. There was a Yankee smartness in the man which was irritated at the idea of being dominated by a person dead for three hundred years; like Mark Twain, he wanted a fresher corpse.

These two motives there were, but they were small compared with the other. It was the third part of him, the Puritan, that was really at war with Shakespeare. He denounced that playwright almost exactly as any contemporary Puritan coming out of a conventicle in a steeple-crowned hat and stiff bands might have denounced the playwright coming out of the stage door of the old Globe Theatre. This is not a mere fancy; it is philosophically true. A legend has run round the newspapers that Bernard Shaw offered himself as a better writer than Shakespeare. This is false and quite unjust; Bernard Shaw never said anything of the kind. The writer whom he did say was better than Shakespeare was not himself, but Bunyan. And he justified it by attributing to Bunyan a virile acceptance of life as a high and harsh adventure, while in Shakespeare he saw nothing but profligate pessimism, the vanitas vanitatum of a disappointed voluptuary. According to this view Shakespeare was always saying, "Out, out, brief candle," because his was only a ballroom candle; while Bunyan was seeking to light such a candle as by God's grace should never be put out.

It is odd that Bernard Shaw's chief error or insensibility should have been the instrument of his noblest affirmation. The denunciation of Shakespeare was a mere misunderstanding. But the denunciation of Shakespeare's pessimism was the most splendidly understanding of all his utterances. This is the greatest thing in Shaw, a serious optimism--even a tragic optimism. Life is a thing too glorious to be enjoyed. To be is an exacting and exhausting business; the trumpet though inspiring is terrible. Nothing that he ever wrote is so noble as his simple reference to the sturdy man who stepped up to the Keeper of the Book of Life and said, "Put down my name, Sir." It is true that Shaw called this heroic philosophy by wrong names and buttressed it with false metaphysics; that was the weakness of the age. The temporary decline of theology had involved the neglect of philosophy and all fine thinking; and Bernard Shaw had to find shaky justifications in Schopenhauer for the sons of God shouting for joy. He called it the Will to Live-- a phrase invented by Prussian professors who would like to exist, but can't. Afterwards he asked people to worship the Life-Force; as if one could worship a hyphen. But though he covered it with crude new names (which are now fortunately crumbling everywhere like bad mortar) he was on the side of the good old cause; the oldest and the best of all causes, the cause of creation against destruction, the cause of yes against no, the cause of the seed against the stony earth and the star against the abyss.

His misunderstanding of Shakespeare arose largely from the fact that he is a Puritan, while Shakespeare was spiritually a Catholic. The former is always screwing himself up to see truth; the latter is often content that truth is there. The Puritan is only strong enough to stiffen; the Catholic is strong enough to relax. Shaw, I think, has entirely misunderstood the pessimistic passages of Shakespeare. They are flying moods which a man with a fixed faith can afford to entertain. That all is vanity, that life is dust and love is ashes, these are frivolities, these are jokes that a Catholic can afford to utter. He knows well enough that there is a life that is not dust and a love that is not ashes. But just as he may let himself go more than the Puritan in the matter of enjoyment, so he may let himself go more than the Puritan in the matter of melancholy. The sad exuberances of Hamlet are merely like the glad exuberances of Falstaff. This is not conjecture; it is the text of Shakespeare. In the very act of uttering his pessimism, Hamlet admits that it is a mood and not the truth. Heaven is a heavenly thing, only to him it seems a foul congregation of vapours. Man is the paragon of animals, only to him he seems a quintessence of dust. Hamlet is quite the reverse of a sceptic. He is a man whose strong intellect believes much more than his weak temperament can make vivid to him. But this power of knowing a thing without feeling it, this power of believing a thing without experiencing it, this is an old Catholic complexity, and the Puritan has never understood it. Shakespeare confesses his moods (mostly by the mouths of villains and failures), but he never sets up his moods against his mind. His cry of vanitas vanitatum is itself only a harmless vanity. Readers may not agree with my calling him Catholic with a big C; but they will hardly complain of my calling him catholic with a small one. And that is here the principal point. Shakespeare was not in any sense a pessimist; he was, if anything, an optimist so universal as to be able to enjoy even pessimism. And this is exactly where he differs from the Puritan. The true Puritan is not squeamish: the true Puritan is free to say "Damn it!" But the Catholic Elizabethan was free (on passing provocation) to say "Damn it all!"

It need hardly be explained that Bernard Shaw added to his negative case of a dramatist to be depreciated a corresponding affirmative case of a dramatist to be exalted and advanced. He was not content with so remote a comparison as that between Shakespeare and Bunyan. In his vivacious weekly articles in the Saturday Review, the real comparison upon which everything turned was the comparison between Shakespeare and Ibsen. He early threw himself with all possible eagerness into the public disputes about the great Scandinavian; and though there was no doubt whatever about which side he supported, there was much that was individual in the line he took. It is not our business here to explore that extinct volcano. You may say that anti-Ibsenism is dead, or you may say that Ibsen is dead; in any case, that controversy is dead, and death, as the Roman poet says, can alone confess of what small atoms we are made. The opponents of Ibsen largely exhibited the permanent qualities of the populace; that is, their instincts were right and their reasons wrong. They made the complete controversial mistake of calling Ibsen a pessimist; whereas, indeed, his chief weakness is a rather childish confidence in mere nature and freedom, and a blindness (either of experience or of culture) in the matter of original sin. In this sense Ibsen is not so much a pessimist as a highly crude kind of optimist. Nevertheless the man in the street was right in his fundamental instinct, as he always is. Ibsen, in his pale northern style, is an optimist; but for all that he is a depressing person. The optimism of Ibsen is less comforting than the pessimism of Dante; just as a Norwegian sunrise, however splendid, is colder than a southern night.

But on the side of those who fought for Ibsen there was also a disagreement, and perhaps also a mistake. The vague army of "the advanced" (an army which advances in all directions) were united in feeling that they ought to be the friends of Ibsen because he also was advancing somewhere somehow. But they were also seriously impressed by Flaubert, by Oscar Wilde and all the rest who told them that a work of art was in another universe from ethics and social good. Therefore many, I think most, of the Ibsenites praised the Ibsen plays merely as choses vues, aesthetic affirmations of what can be without any reference to what ought to be. Mr. William Archer himself inclined to this view, though his strong sagacity kept him in a haze of healthy doubt on the subject. Mr. Walkley certainly took this view. But this view Mr. George Bernard Shaw abruptly and violently refused to take.

With the full Puritan combination of passion and precision he informed everybody that Ibsen was not artistic, but moral; that his dramas were didactic, that all great art was didactic, that Ibsen was strongly on the side of some of his characters and strongly against others, that there was preaching and public spirit in the work of good dramatists; and that if this were not so, dramatists and all other artists would be mere panders of intellectual debauchery, to be locked up as the Puritans locked up the stage players. No one can understand Bernard Shaw who does not give full value to this early revolt of his on behalf of ethics against the ruling school of l'art pour l'art. It is interesting because it is connected with other ambitions in the man, especially with that which has made him somewhat vainer of being a Parish Councillor than of being one of the most popular dramatists in Europe. But its chief interest is again to be referred to our stratification of the psychology; it is the lover of true things rebelling for once against merely new things; it is the Puritan suddenly refusing to be the mere Progressive.

But this attitude obviously laid on the ethical lover of Ibsen a not inconsiderable obligation. If the new drama had an ethical purpose, what was it? and if Ibsen was a moral teacher, what the deuce was he teaching? Answers to this question, answers of manifold brilliancy and promise, were scattered through all the dramatic criticisms of those years on the Saturday Review. But even Bernard Shaw grew tired after a time of discussing Ibsen only in connection with the current pantomime or the latest musical comedy. It was felt that so much sincerity and fertility of explanation justified a concentrated attack; and in 1891 appeared the brilliant book called The Quintessence of

Ibsenism, which some have declared to be merely the quintessence of Shaw. However this may be, it was in fact and profession the quintessence of Shaw's theory of the morality or propaganda of Ibsen.

The book itself is much longer than the book that I am writing; and as is only right in so spirited an apologist, every paragraph is provocative. I could write an essay on every sentence which I accept and three essays on every sentence which I deny. Bernard Shaw himself is a master of compression; he can put a conception more compactly than any other man alive. It is therefore rather difficult to compress his compression; one feels as if one were trying to extract a beef essence from Bovril. But the shortest form in which I can state the idea of _The Quintessence of Ibsenism_ is that it is the idea of distrusting ideals, which are universal, in comparison with facts, which are miscellaneous. The man whom he attacks throughout he calls "The Idealist"; that is the man who permits himself to be mainly moved by a moral generalisation. "Actions," he says, "are to be judged by their effect on happiness, and not by their conformity to any ideal." As we have already seen, there is a certain inconsistency here; for while Shaw had always chucked all ideals overboard the one he had chucked first was the ideal of happiness. Passing this however for the present, we may mark the above as the most satisfying summary. If I tell a lie I am not to blame myself for having violated the ideal of truth, but only for having perhaps got myself into a mess and made things worse than they were before. If I have broken my word I need not feel (as my fathers did) that I have broken something inside of me, as one who breaks a blood vessel. It all depends on whether I have broken up something outside me; as one who breaks up an evening party. If I shoot my father the only question is whether I have made him happy. I must not admit the idealistic conception that the mere shooting of my father might possibly make me unhappy. We are to judge of every individual case as it arises, apparently without any social summary or moral ready-reckoner at all. "The Golden Rule is that there is no Golden Rule." We must not say that it is right to keep promises, but that it may be right to keep this promise. Essentially it is anarchy; nor is it very easy to see how a state could be very comfortable which was Socialist in all its public morality and Anarchist in all its private. But if it is anarchy, it is anarchy without any of the abandon and exuberance of anarchy. It is a worried and conscientious anarchy; an anarchy of painful delicacy and even caution. For it refuses to trust in traditional experiments or plainly trodden tracks; every case must be considered anew from the beginning, and yet considered with the most wide-eyed care for human welfare; every man must act as if he were the first man made. Briefly, we must always be worrying about what is best for our children, and we must not take one hint or rule of thumb from our fathers. Some think that this anarchism would make a man tread down mighty cities in his madness. I think it would make a man walk down the street as if he were walking on egg-shells. I do not think this experiment in opportunism would end in frantic license; I think it would end in frozen timidity. If a man was forbidden to solve moral problems by moral science or the help of mankind, his course would be quite easy--he would not solve the problems. The world instead of being a knot so tangled as to need unravelling, would simply become a piece of clock-work too complicated to be touched. I cannot think that this untutored worry was what Ibsen meant; I have my doubts as to whether it was what Shaw meant; but I do not think that it can be substantially doubted that it was what he said.

In any case it can be asserted that the general aim of the work was to exalt the immediate conclusions of practice against the general conclusions of theory. Shaw objected to the solution of every problem in a play being by its nature a general solution, applicable to all other such problems. He disliked the entrance of a universal justice at the end of the last act; treading down all the personal ultimatums and all the varied certainties of men. He disliked the god from the machine--because he was from a machine. But even without the machine he tended to dislike the god; because a god is more general than a man. His enemies have accused Shaw of being anti-domestic, a shaker of the roof-tree. But in this sense Shaw may be called almost madly domestic. He wishes each private problem to be settled in private, without reference to sociological ethics. And the only objection to this kind of gigantic casuistry is that the theatre is really too small to discuss it. It would not be fair to play David and Goliath on a stage too small to admit Goliath. And it is not fair to discuss private morality on a stage too small to admit the enormous presence of public morality; that character which has not appeared in a play since the Middle Ages; whose name is Everyman and whose honour we have all in our keeping.

* * * *

The Dramatist

NO one who was alive at the time and interested in such matters will ever forget the first acting of Arms and the Man. It was applauded by that indescribable element in all of us which rejoices to see the genuine thing prevail against the plausible; that element which rejoices that even its enemies are alive. Apart from the problems raised in the play, the very form of it was an attractive and forcible innovation. Classic plays which were wholly heroic, comic plays which were wholly and even heartlessly ironical, were common enough. Commonest of all in this particular time was the play that began playfully, with plenty of comic business, and was gradually sobered by sentiment until it ended on a note of romance or even of pathos. A commonplace little officer, the butt of the mess, becomes by the last act as high and hopeless a lover as Dante. Or a vulgar and violent pork-butcher remembers his own youth before the curtain goes down. The first thing that Bernard Shaw did when he stepped before the footlights was to reverse this process. He resolved to build a play not on pathos, but on bathos. The officer should be heroic first and then everyone should laugh at him; the curtain should go up on a man remembering his youth, and he should only reveal himself as a violent pork-butcher when someone interrupted him with an order for pork. This merely technical originality is indicated in the very title of the play. The Arma Virumque of Virgil is a mounting and ascending phrase, the man is more than his weapons. The Latin line suggests a superb procession which should bring on to the stage the brazen and resounding armour, the shield and shattering axe, but end with the hero himself, taller and more terrible because unarmed. The technical effect of Shaw's scheme is like the same scene, in which a crowd should carry even more gigantic shapes of shield and helmet, but when the horns and howls were at their highest, should end with the figure of Little Tich. The name itself is meant to be a bathos; arms--and the man.

It is well to begin with the superficial; and this is the superficial effectiveness of Shaw; the brilliancy of bathos. But of course the vitality and value of his plays does not lie merely in this; any more than the value of Swinburne lies in alliteration or the value of Hood in puns. This is not his message; but it is his method; it is his style. The first taste we had of it was in this play of Arms and the Man; but even at the very first it was evident that there was much more in the play than that. Among other things there was one thing not unimportant; there was savage sincerity. Indeed, only a ferociously sincere person can produce such effective flippancies on a matter like war; just as only a strong man could juggle with cannon balls. It is all very well to use the word "fool" as synonymous with "jester"; but daily experience shows that it is generally the solemn and silent man who is the fool. It is all very well to accuse Mr. Shaw of standing on his head; but if you stand on your head you must have a hard and solid head to stand on. In Arms and the Man the bathos of form was strictly the incarnation of a strong satire in the idea. The play opens in an atmosphere of military melodrama; the dashing officer of cavalry going off to death in an attitude, the lovely heroine left in tearful rapture; the brass band, the noise of guns and the red fire. Into all this enters Bluntschli, the little sturdy crop-haired Swiss professional soldier, a man without a country but with a trade. He tells the army-adoring heroine frankly that she is a humbug; and she, after a moment's reflection, appears to agree with him. The play is like nearly all Shaw's plays, the dialogue of a conversion. By the end of it the young lady has lost all her military illusions and admires this mercenary soldier not because he faces guns, but because he faces facts.

This was a fitting entrance for Shaw to his didactic drama; because the commonplace courage which he respects in Bluntschli was the one virtue which he was destined to praise throughout. We can best see how the play symbolises and summarises Bernard Shaw if we compare it with some other attack by modern humanitarians upon war. Shaw has many of the actual opinions of Tolstoy. Like Tolstoy he tells men, with coarse innocence, that romantic war is only butchery and that romantic love is only lust. But Tolstoy objects to these things because they are real; he really wishes to abolish them. Shaw only objects to them in so far as they are ideal; that is in so far as they are idealised. Shaw objects not so much to war as to the attractiveness of war. He does not so much dislike love as the love of love. Before the temple of Mars, Tolstoy stands and thunders, "There shall be no wars"; Bernard Shaw merely murmurs, "Wars if you must; but for God's sake, not war songs." Before the temple of Venus, Tolstoy cries terribly, "Come out of it!"; Shaw is quite content to say, "Do not be taken in by it." Tolstoy seems really to propose that high passion and patriotic valour should be destroyed. Shaw is more moderate; and only asks that they should be desecrated. Upon this note, both about sex and conflict, he was destined to dwell through much of his work with the most wonderful variations of witty adventure and intellectual surprise. It may be doubted perhaps whether this realism in love and war is quite so sensible as it looks. Securus judicat orbis terrarum; the world is wiser than the moderns. The world has kept sentimentalities simply because they are the most practical things in the world. They alone make men do things. The world does not encourage a quite rational lover, simply because a perfectly rational lover would never get married. The world does not encourage a perfectly rational army, because a perfectly rational army would run away.

The brain of Bernard Shaw was like a wedge in the literal sense. Its sharpest end was always in front; and it split our society from end to end the moment it had entrance at all. As I have said he was long unheard of; but he had not the tragedy of many authors, who were heard of long before they were heard. When you had read any Shaw you read all Shaw. When you had seen one of his plays you waited for more. And when he brought them out in volume form, you did what is repugnant to any literary man-- you bought a book.

The dramatic volume with which Shaw dazzled the public was called, Plays, Pleasant and Unpleasant. I think the most striking and typical thing about it was that he did not know very clearly which plays were unpleasant and which were pleasant. "Pleasant" is a word which is almost unmeaning to Bernard Shaw. Except, as I suppose, in music (where I cannot follow him), relish and receptivity are things that simply do not appear. He has the best of tongues and the worst of palates. With the possible exception of _Mrs. Warren's Profession_ (which was at least unpleasant in the sense of being forbidden) I can see no particular reason why any of the seven plays should be held specially to please or displease. First in fame and contemporary importance came the reprint of _Arms and the Man,_ of which I have already spoken. Over all the rest towered unquestionably the two figures of Mrs. Warren and of Candida. They were neither of them pleasant, except as all good art is pleasant. They were neither of them really unpleasant except as all truth is unpleasant. But they did represent the author's normal preference and his principal fear; and those two sculptured giantesses largely upheld his fame.

I fancy that the author rather dislikes Candida because it is so generally liked. I give my own feeling for what it is worth (a foolish phrase), but I think that there were only two moments when this powerful writer was truly, in the ancient and popular sense, inspired; that is, breathing from a bigger self and telling more truth than he knew. One is that scene in a later play where after the secrets and revenges of Egypt have rioted and rotted all round him, the colossal sanity of Caesar is suddenly acclaimed with swords. The other is that great last scene in Candida where the wife, stung into final speech, declared her purpose of remaining with the strong man because he is the weak man. The wife is asked to decide between two men, one a strenuous self-confident popular preacher, her husband, the other a wild and weak young poet, logically futile and physically timid, her lover; and she chooses the former because he has more weakness and more need of her. Even among the plain and ringing paradoxes of the Shaw play this is one of the best reversals or turnovers ever effected. A paradoxical writer like Bernard Shaw is perpetually and tiresomely told that he stands on his head. But all romance and all religion consist in making the whole universe stand on its head. That reversal is the whole idea of virtue; that the last shall be first and the first last. Considered as a pure piece of Shaw therefore, the thing is of the best. But it is also something much better than Shaw. The writer touches certain realities commonly outside his scope; especially the reality of the normal wife's attitude to the normal husband, an attitude which is not romantic but which is yet quite quixotic; which is insanely unselfish and yet quite cynically clear-sighted. It involves human sacrifice without in the least involving idolatry.

The truth is that in this place Bernard Shaw comes within an inch of expressing something that is not properly expressed anywhere else; the idea of marriage. Marriage is not a mere chain upon love as the anarchists say; nor is it a mere crown upon love as the sentimentalists say. Marriage is a fact, an actual human relation like that of motherhood which has certain human habits and loyalties, except in a few monstrous cases where it is turned to torture by special insanity and sin. A marriage is neither an ecstasy nor a slavery; it is a commonwealth; it is a separate working and fighting thing like a nation. Kings and diplomatists talk of "forming alliances" when they make weddings; but indeed every wedding is primarily an alliance. The family is a fact even when it is not an agreeable fact, and a man is part of his wife even when he wishes he wasn't. The twain are one flesh--yes, even when they are not one spirit. Man is duplex. Man is a quadruped.

Of this ancient and essential relation there are certain emotional results, which are subtle, like all the growths of nature. And one of them is the attitude of the wife to the husband, whom she regards at once as the strongest and most helpless of human figures. She regards him in some strange fashion at once as a warrior who must make his way and as an infant who is sure to lose his way. The man has emotions which exactly correspond; sometimes looking down at his wife and sometimes up at her; for marriage is like a splendid game of see-saw. Whatever else it is, it is not comradeship. This living, ancestral bond (not of love or fear, but strictly of marriage) has been twice expressed splendidly in literature. The man's incurable sense of the mother in his lawful wife was uttered by Browning in one of his two or three truly shattering lines of genius, when he makes the execrable Guido fall back finally upon the fact of marriage and the wife whom he has trodden like mire:

"Christ! Maria! God, Pompilia, will you let them murder me?"

And the woman's witness to the same fact has been best expressed by Bernard Shaw in this great scene where she remains with the great stalwart successful public man because he is really too little to run alone.

There are one or two errors in the play; and they are all due to the primary error of despising the mental attitude of romance, which is the only key to real human conduct. For instance, the love making of the young poet is all wrong. He is supposed to be a romantic and amorous boy; and therefore the dramatist tries to make him talk turgidly, about seeking for "an archangel with purple wings" who shall be worthy of his lady. But a lad in love would never talk in this mock heroic style; there is no period at which the young male is more sensitive and serious and afraid of looking a fool. This is a blunder; but there is another much bigger and blacker. It is completely and disastrously false to the whole nature of falling in love to make the young Eugene complain of the cruelty which makes Candida defile her fair hands with domestic duties. No boy in love with a beautiful woman would ever feel disgusted when she peeled potatoes or trimmed lamps. He would like her to be domestic. He would simply feel that the potatoes had become poetical and the lamps gained an extra light. This may be irrational; but we are not talking of rationality, but of the psychology of first love. It may be very unfair to women that the toil and triviality of potato peeling should be seen through a glamour of romance; but the glamour is quite as certain a fact as the potatoes. It may be a bad thing in sociology that men should deify domesticity in girls as something dainty and magical; but all men do. Personally I do not think it a bad thing at all; but that is another argument. The argument here is that Bernard Shaw, in aiming at mere realism, makes a big mistake in reality. Misled by his great heresy of looking at emotions from the outside, he makes Eugene a cold-blooded prig at the very moment when he is trying, for his own dramatic purposes, to make him a hot-blooded lover. He makes the young lover an idealistic theoriser about the very things about which he really would have been a sort of mystical materialist. Here the romantic Irishman is much more right than the very rational one; and there is far more truth to life as it is in Lover's couplet--

"And envied the chicken That Peggy was pickin'."

than in Eugene's solemn, aesthetic protest against the potato-skins and the lamp-oil. For dramatic purposes, G. B. S., even if he despises romance, ought to comprehend it. But then, if once he comprehended romance, he would not despise it.

The series contained, besides its more substantial work, tragic and comic, a comparative frivolity called The Man of Destiny. It is a little comedy about Napoleon, and is chiefly interesting as a foreshadowing of his after sketches of heroes and strong men; it is a kind of parody of Caesar and Cleopatra before it was written. In this connection the mere title of this Napoleonic play is of interest. All Shaw's generation and school of thought remembered Napoleon only by his late and corrupt title of "The Man of Destiny," a title only given to him when he was already fat and tired and destined to exile. They forgot that through all the really thrilling and creative part of his career he was not the man of destiny, but the man who defied destiny. Shaw's sketch is extraordinarily clever; but it is tinged with this unmilitary notion of an inevitable conquest; and this we must remember when we come to those larger canvases on which he painted his more serious heroes. As for the play, it is packed with good things, of which the last is perhaps the best. The long duologue between Bonaparte and the Irish lady ends with the General declaring that he will only be beaten when he meets an English army under an Irish general. It has always been one of Shaw's paradoxes that the English mind has the force to fulfil orders, while the Irish mind has the intelligence to give them, and it is among those of his paradoxes which contain a certain truth.

A far more important play is The Philanderer, an ironic comedy which is full of fine strokes and real satire; it is more especially the vehicle of some of Shaw's best satire upon physical science. Nothing could be cleverer than the picture of the young, strenuous doctor, in the utter innocence of his professional ambition, who has discovered a new disease, and is delighted when he finds people suffering from it and cast down to despair when he finds that it does not exist. The point is worth a pause, because it is a good, short way of stating Shaw's attitude, right or wrong, upon the whole of formal morality. What he dislikes in young Doctor Paramore is that he has interposed a secondary and false conscience between himself and the facts. When his disease is disproved, instead of seeing the escape of a human being who thought he was going to die of it, Paramore sees the downfall of a kind of flag or cause. This is the whole contention of The Quintessence of Ibsenism, put better than the book puts it; it is a really sharp exposition of the dangers of "idealism," the sacrifice of people to principles, and Shaw is even wiser in his suggestion that this excessive idealism exists nowhere so strongly as in the world of physical science. He shows that the scientist tends to be more concerned about the sickness than about the sick man; but it was certainly in his mind to suggest here also that the idealist is more concerned about the sin than about the sinner.

This business of Dr. Paramore's disease while it is the most farcical thing in the play is also the most philosophic and important. The rest of the figures, including the Philanderer himself, are in the full sense of those blasting and obliterating words "funny without being vulgar," that is, funny without being of any importance to the masses of men. It is a play about a dashing and advanced "Ibsen Club," and the squabble between the young Ibsenites and the old people who are not yet up to Ibsen. It would be hard to find a stronger example of Shaw's only essential error, modernity--which means the seeking for truth in terms of time. Only a few years have passed and already almost half the wit of that wonderful play is wasted, because it all turns on the newness of a fashion that is no longer new. Doubtless many people still think the Ibsen drama a great thing, like the French classical drama. But going to "The Philanderer" is like going among periwigs and rapiers and hearing that the young men are now all for Racine. What makes such work sound unreal is not the praise of Ibsen, but the praise of the novelty of Ibsen. Any advantage that Bernard Shaw had over Colonel Craven I have over Bernard Shaw; we who happen to be born last have the meaningless and paltry triumph in that meaningless and paltry war. We are the superiors by that silliest and most snobbish of all superiorities, the mere aristocracy of time. All works must become thus old and insipid which have ever tried to be "modern," which have consented to smell of time rather than of eternity. Only those who have stooped to be in advance of their time will ever find themselves behind it.

But it is irritating to think what diamonds, what dazzling silver of Shavian wit has been sunk in such an out-of-date warship. In The Philanderer there are five hundred excellent and about five magnificent things. The rattle of repartees between the doctor and the soldier about the humanity of their two trades is admirable. Or again, when the colonel tells Chartaris that "in his young days" he would have no more behaved like Chartaris than he would have cheated at cards. After a pause Chartaris says, "You're getting old, Craven, and you make a virtue of it as usual." And there is an altitude of aerial tragedy in the words of Grace, who has refused the man she loves, to Julia, who is marrying the man she doesn't, "This is what they call a happy ending-- these men."

There is an acrid taste in The Philanderer; and certainly he might be considered a super-sensitive person who should find anything acrid in You Never Can Tell. This play is the nearest approach to frank and objectless exuberance in the whole of Shaw's work. Punch, with wisdom as well as wit, said that it might well be called not "You Never Can Tell" but "You Never Can be Shaw." And yet if anyone will read this blazing farce and then after it any of the romantic farces, such as Pickwick or even The Wrong Box, I do not think he will be disposed to erase or even to modify what I said at the beginning about the ingrained grimness and even inhumanity of Shaw's art. To take but one test: love, in an "extravaganza," may be light love or love in idleness, but it should be hearty and happy love if it is to add to the general hilarity. Such are the ludicrous but lucky love affairs of the sportsman Winkle and the Maestro Jimson. In Gloria's collapse before her bullying lover there is something at once cold and unclean; it calls up all the modern supermen with their cruel and fishy eyes. Such farces should begin in a friendly air, in a tavern. There is something very symbolic of Shaw in the fact that his farce begins in a dentist's.

The only one out of this brilliant batch of plays in which I think that the method adopted really fails, is the one called Widower's Houses. The best touch of Shaw is simply in the title. The simple substitution of widowers for widows contains almost the whole bitter and yet boisterous protest of Shaw; all his preference for undignified fact over dignified phrase; all his dislike of those subtle trends of sex or mystery which swing the logician off the straight line. We can imagine him crying, "Why in the name of death and conscience should it be tragic to be a widow but comic to be a widower?" But the rationalistic method is here applied quite wrong as regards the production of a drama. The most dramatic point in the affair is when the open and indecent rack-renter turns on the decent young man of means and proves to him that he is equally guilty, that he also can only grind his corn by grinding the faces of the poor. But even here the point is undramatic because it is indirect; it is indirect because it is merely sociological. It may be the truth that a young man living on an unexamined income which ultimately covers a great deal of house-property is as dangerous as any despot or thief. But it is a truth that you can no more put into a play than into a triolet. You can make a play out of one man robbing another man, but not out of one man robbing a million men; still less out of his robbing them unconsciously.

Of the plays collected in this book I have kept _Mrs. Warren's Profession_ to the last, because, fine as it is, it is even finer and more important because of its fate, which was to rouse a long and serious storm and to be vetoed by the Censor of Plays. I say that this drama is most important because of the quarrel that came out of it. If I were speaking of some mere artist this might be an insult. But there are high and heroic things in Bernard Shaw; and one of the highest and most heroic is this, that he certainly cares much more for a quarrel than for a play. And this quarrel about the censorship is one on which he feels so strongly that in a book embodying any sort of sympathy it would be much better to leave out Mrs. Warren than to leave out Mr. Redford. The veto was the pivot of so very personal a movement by the dramatist, of so very positive an assertion of his own attitude towards things, that it is only just and necessary to state what were the two essential parties to the dispute; the play and the official who prevented the play.

The play of Mrs. Warren's Profession is concerned with a coarse mother and a cold daughter; the mother drives the ordinary and dirty trade of harlotry; the daughter does not know until the end the atrocious origin of all her own comfort and refinement. The daughter, when the discovery is made, freezes up into an iceberg of contempt; which is indeed a very womanly thing to do. The mother explodes into pulverising cynicism and practicality; which is also very womanly. The dialogue is drastic and sweeping; the daughter says the trade is loathsome; the mother answers that she loathes it herself; that every healthy person does loathe the trade by which she lives. And beyond question the general effect of the play is that the trade is loathsome; supposing anyone to be so insensible as to require to be told of the fact. Undoubtedly the upshot is that a brothel is a miserable business, and a brothel-keeper a miserable woman.

The whole dramatic art of Shaw is in the literal sense of the word, tragi-comic; I mean that the comic part comes after the tragedy. But just as You Never Can Tell represents the nearest approach of Shaw to the purely comic, so Mrs. Warren's Profession represents his only complete, or nearly complete, tragedy. There is no twopenny modernism in it, as in The Philanderer. Mrs. Warren is as old as the Old Testament; "for she hath cast down many wounded, yea, many strong men have been slain by her; her house is in the gates of hell, going down into the chamber of death." Here is no subtle ethics, as in Widowers' Houses; for even those moderns who think it noble that a woman should throw away her honour, surely cannot think it especially noble that she should sell it. Here is no lighting up by laughter, astonishment, and happy coincidence, as in You Never Can Tell. The play is a pure tragedy about a permanent and quite plain human problem; the problem is as plain and permanent, the tragedy is as proud and pure, as in Oedipus or Macbeth. This play was presented in the ordinary way for public performance and was suddenly stopped by the Censor of Plays.

The Censor of Plays is a small and accidental eighteenth-century official. Like nearly all the powers which Englishmen now respect as ancient and rooted, he is very recent. Novels and newspapers still talk of the English aristocracy that came over with William the Conqueror. Little of our effective oligarchy is as old as the Reformation; and none of it came over with William the Conqueror. Some of the older English landlords came over with William of Orange; the rest have come by ordinary alien immigration. In the same way we always talk of the Victorian woman (with her smelling salts and sentiment) as the old-fashioned woman. But she really was a quite new-fashioned woman; she considered herself, and was, an advance in delicacy and civilisation upon the coarse and candid Elizabethan woman to whom we are now returning. We are never oppressed by old things; it is recent things that can really oppress. And in accordance with this principle modern England has accepted, as if it were a part of perennial morality, a tenth-rate job of Walpole's worst days called the Censorship of the Drama. Just as they have supposed the eighteenth-century parvenus to date from Hastings, just as they have supposed the eighteenth-century ladies to date from Eve, so they have supposed the eighteenth-century Censorship to date from Sinai. The origin of the thing was in truth purely political. Its first and principal achievement was to prevent Fielding from writing plays; not at all because the plays were coarse, but because they criticised the Government. Fielding was a free writer; but they did not resent his sexual freedom; the Censor would not have objected if he had torn away the most intimate curtains of decency or rent the last rag from private life. What the Censor disliked was his rending the curtain from public life. There is still much of that spirit in our country; there are no affairs which men seek so much to cover up as public affairs. But the thing was done somewhat more boldly and baldly in Walpole's day; and the Censorship of plays has its origin, not merely in tyranny, but in a quite trifling and temporary and partisan piece of tyranny; a thing in its nature far more ephemeral, far less essential, than Ship Money. Perhaps its brightest moment was when the office of censor was held by that filthy writer, Colman the younger; and when he gravely refused to license a work by the author of Our Village. Few funnier notions can ever have actually been facts than this notion that the restraint and chastity of George Colman saved the English public from the eroticism and obscenity of Miss Mitford.

Such was the play; and such was the power that stopped the play. A private man wrote it; another private man forbade it; nor was there any difference between Mr. Shaw's authority and Mr. Redford's, except that Mr. Shaw did defend his action on public grounds and Mr. Redford did not. The dramatist had simply been suppressed by a despot; and what was worse (because it was modern) by a silent and evasive despot; a despot in hiding. People talk about the pride of tyrants; but we at the present day suffer from the modesty of tyrants; from the shyness and the shrinking secrecy of the strong. Shaw's preface to _Mrs. Warren's Profession_ was far more fit to be called a public document than the slovenly refusal of the individual official; it had more exactness, more universal application, more authority. Shaw on Redford was far more national and responsible than Redford on Shaw.

The dramatist found in the quarrel one of the important occasions of his life, because the crisis called out something in him which is in many ways his highest quality--righteous indignation. As a mere matter of the art of controversy of course he carried the war into the enemy's camp at once. He did not linger over loose excuses for licence; he declared at once that the Censor was licentious, while he, Bernard Shaw, was clean. He did not discuss whether a Censorship ought to make the drama moral. He declared that it made the drama immoral. With a fine strategic audacity he attacked the Censor quite as much for what he permitted as for what he prevented. He charged him with encouraging all plays that attracted men to vice and only stopping those which discouraged them from it. Nor was this attitude by any means an idle paradox. Many plays appear (as Shaw pointed out) in which the prostitute and the procuress are practically obvious, and in which they are represented as revelling in beautiful surroundings and basking in brilliant popularity. The crime of Shaw was not that he introduced the Gaiety Girl; that had been done, with little enough decorum, in a hundred musical comedies. The crime of Shaw was that he introduced the Gaiety Girl, but did not represent her life as all gaiety. The pleasures of vice were already flaunted before the playgoers. It was the perils of vice that were carefully concealed from them. The gay adventures, the gorgeous dresses, the champagne and oysters, the diamonds and motor-cars, dramatists were allowed to drag all these dazzling temptations before any silly housemaid in the gallery who was grumbling at her wages. But they were not allowed to warn her of the vulgarity and the nausea, the dreary deceptions and the blasting diseases of that life. Mrs. Warren's Profession was not up to a sufficient standard of immorality; it was not spicy enough to pass the Censor. The acceptable and the accepted plays were those which made the fall of a woman fashionable and fascinating; for all the world as if the Censor's profession were the same as Mrs. Warren's profession.

Such was the angle of Shaw's energetic attack; and it is not to be denied that there was exaggeration in it, and what is so much worse, omission. The argument might easily be carried too far; it might end with a scene of screaming torture in the Inquisition as a corrective to the too amiable view of a clergyman in The Private Secretary. But the controversy is definitely worth recording, if only as an excellent example of the author's aggressive attitude and his love of turning the tables in debate. Moreover, though this point of view involves a potential overstatement, it also involves an important truth. One of the best points urged in the course of it was this, that though vice is punished in conventional drama, the punishment is not really impressive, because it is not inevitable or even probable. It does not arise out of the evil act. Years afterwards Bernard Shaw urged this argument again in connection with his friend Mr. Granville Barker's play of Waste, in which the woman dies from an illegal operation. Bernard Shaw said, truly enough, that if she had died from poison or a pistol shot it would have left everyone unmoved, for pistols do not in their nature follow female unchastity. Illegal operations very often do. The punishment was one which might follow the crime, not only in that case, but in many cases. Here, I think, the whole argument might be sufficiently cleared up by saying that the objection to such things on the stage is a purely artistic objection. There is nothing wrong in talking about an illegal operation; there are plenty of occasions when it would be very wrong not to talk about it. But it may easily be just a shade too ugly for the shape of any work of art. There is nothing wrong about being sick; but if Bernard Shaw wrote a play in which all the characters expressed their dislike of animal food by vomiting on the stage, I think we should be justified in saying that the thing was outside, not the laws of morality, but the framework of civilised literature. The instinctive movement of repulsion which everyone has when hearing of the operation in Waste is not an ethical repulsion at all. But it is an aesthetic repulsion, and a right one.

But I have only dwelt on this particular fighting phase because it leaves us facing the ultimate characteristics which I mentioned first. Bernard Shaw cares nothing for art; in comparison with morals, literally nothing. Bernard Shaw is a Puritan and his work is Puritan work. He has all the essentials of the old, virile and extinct Protestant type. In his work he is as ugly as a Puritan. He is as indecent as a Puritan. He is as full of gross words and sensual facts as a sermon of the seventeenth century. Up to this point of his life indeed hardly anyone would have dreamed of calling him a Puritan; he was called sometimes an anarchist, sometimes a buffoon, sometimes (by the more discerning stupid people) a prig. His attitude towards current problems was felt to be arresting and even indecent; I do not think that anyone thought of connecting it with the old Calvinistic morality. But Shaw, who knew better than the Shavians, was at this moment on the very eve of confessing his moral origin. The next book of plays he produced (including The Devil's Disciple, Captain Brassbound's Conversion, and Caesar and Cleopatra), actually bore the title of Plays for Puritans.

The play called The Devil's Disciple has great merits, but the merits are incidental. Some of its jokes are serious and important, but its general plan can only be called a joke. Almost alone among Bernard Shaw's plays (except of course such things as How he Lied to her Husband and The Admirable Bashville) this drama does not turn on any very plain pivot of ethical or philosophical conviction. The artistic idea seems to be the notion of a melodrama in which all the conventional melodramatic situations shall suddenly take unconventional turns. Just where the melodramatic clergyman would show courage he appears to show cowardice; just where the melodramatic sinner would confess his love he confesses his indifference. This is a little too like the Shaw of the newspaper critics rather than the Shaw of reality. There are indeed present in the play two of the writer's principal moral conceptions. The first is the idea of a great heroic action coming in a sense from nowhere; that is, not coming from any commonplace motive; being born in the soul in naked beauty, coming with its own authority and testifying only to itself. Shaw's agent does not act towards something, but from something. The hero dies, not because he desires heroism, but because he has it. So in this particular play the Devil's Disciple finds that his own nature will not permit him to put the rope around another man's neck; he has no reasons of desire, affection, or even equity; his death is a sort of divine whim. And in connection with this the dramatist introduces another favourite moral; the objection to perpetual playing upon the motive of sex. He deliberately lures the onlooker into the net of Cupid in order to tell him with salutary decision that Cupid is not there at all. Millions of melodramatic dramatists have made a man face death for the woman he loves; Shaw makes him face death for the woman he does not love--merely in order to put woman in her place. He objects to that idolatry of sexualism which makes it the fountain of all forcible enthusiasms; he dislikes the amorous drama which makes the female the only key to the male. He is Feminist in politics, but Anti-feminist in emotion. His key to most problems is, "Ne cherchez pas la femme."

As has been observed, the incidental felicities of the play are frequent and memorable, especially those connected with the character of General Burgoyne, the real full-blooded, free-thinking eighteenth century gentleman, who was much too much of an aristocrat not to be a liberal. One of the best thrusts in all the Shavian fencing matches is that which occurs when Richard Dudgeon, condemned to be hanged, asks rhetorically why he cannot be shot like a soldier. "Now there you speak like a civilian," replies General Burgoyne. "Have you formed any conception of the condition of marksmanship in the British Army?" Excellent, too, is the passage in which his subordinate speaks of crushing the enemy in America, and Burgoyne asks him who will crush their enemies in England, snobbery and jobbery and incurable carelessness and sloth. And in one sentence towards the end, Shaw reaches a wider and more genial comprehension of mankind than he shows anywhere else; "it takes all sorts to make a world, saints as well as soldiers." If Shaw had remembered that sentence on other occasions he would have avoided his mistake about Caesar and Brutus. It is not only true that it takes all sorts to make a world; but the world cannot succeed without its failures. Perhaps the most doubtful point of all in the play is why it is a play for Puritans; except the hideous picture of a Calvinistic home is meant to destroy Puritanism. And indeed in this connection it is constantly necessary to fall back upon the facts of which I have spoken at the beginning of this brief study; it is necessary especially to remember that Shaw could in all probability speak of Puritanism from the inside. In that domestic circle which took him to hear Moody and Sankey, in that domestic circle which was teetotal even when it was intoxicated, in that atmosphere and society Shaw might even have met the monstrous mother in The Devil's Disciple, the horrible old woman who declares that she has hardened her heart to hate her children, because the heart of man is desperately wicked, the old ghoul who has made one of her children an imbecile and the other an outcast. Such types do occur in small societies drunk with the dismal wine of Puritan determinism. It is possible that there were among Irish Calvinists people who denied that charity was a Christian virtue. It is possible that among Puritans there were people who thought a heart was a kind of heart disease. But it is enough to make one tear one's hair to think that a man of genius received his first impressions in so small a corner of Europe that he could for a long time suppose that this Puritanism was current among Christian men. The question, however, need not detain us, for the batch of plays contained two others about which it is easier to speak.

The third play in order in the series called Plays for Puritans is a very charming one; Captain Brassbound's Conversion. This also turns, as does so much of the Caesar drama, on the idea of vanity of revenge-- the idea that it is too slight and silly a thing for a man to allow to occupy and corrupt his consciousness. It is not, of course, the morality that is new here, but the touch of cold laughter in the core of the morality. Many saints and sages have denounced vengeance. But they treated vengeance as something too great for man. "Vengeance is Mine, saith the Lord; I will repay." Shaw treats vengeance as something too small for man--a monkey trick he ought to have outlived, a childish storm of tears which he ought to be able to control. In the story in question Captain Brassbound has nourished through his whole erratic existence, racketting about all the unsavoury parts of Africa--a mission of private punishment which appears to him as a mission of holy justice. His mother has died in consequence of a judge's decision, and Brassbound roams and schemes until the judge falls into his hands. Then a pleasant society lady, Lady Cicely Waynefleet tells him in an easy conversational undertone-- a rivulet of speech which ripples while she is mending his coat-- that he is making a fool of himself, that his wrong is irrelevant, that his vengeance is objectless, that he would be much better if he flung his morbid fancy away for ever; in short, she tells him he is ruining himself for the sake of ruining a total stranger. Here again we have the note of the economist, the hatred of mere loss. Shaw (one might almost say) dislikes murder, not so much because it wastes the life of the corpse as because it wastes the time of the murderer. If he were endeavouring to persuade one of his moon-lighting fellow-countrymen not to shoot his landlord, I can imagine him explaining with benevolent emphasis that it was not so much a question of losing a life as of throwing away a bullet. But indeed the Irish comparison alone suggests a doubt which wriggles in the recesses of my mind about the complete reliability of the philosophy of Lady Cicely Waynefleet, the complete finality of the moral of Captain Brassbound's Conversion. Of course, it was very natural in an aristocrat like Lady Cicely Waynefleet to wish to let sleeping dogs lie, especially those whom Mr. Blatchford calls under-dogs. Of course it was natural for her to wish everything to be smooth and sweet-tempered. But I have the obstinate question in the corner of my brain, whether if a few Captain Brassbounds did revenge themselves on judges, the quality of our judges might not materially improve.

When this doubt is once off one's conscience one can lose oneself in the bottomless beatitude of Lady Cicely Waynefleet, one of the most living and laughing things that her maker has made. I do not know any stronger way of stating the beauty of the character than by saying that it was written specially for Ellen Terry, and that it is, with Beatrice, one of the very few characters in which the dramatist can claim some part of her triumph.

We may now pass to the more important of the plays. For some time Bernard Shaw would seem to have been brooding upon the soul of Julius Caesar. There must always be a strong human curiosity about the soul of Julius Caesar; and, among other things, about whether he had a soul. The conjunction of Shaw and Caesar has about it something smooth and inevitable; for this decisive reason, that Caesar is really the only great man of history to whom the Shaw theories apply. Caesar was a Shaw hero. Caesar was merciful without being in the least pitiful; his mercy was colder than justice. Caesar was a conqueror without being in any hearty sense a soldier; his courage was lonelier than fear. Caesar was a demagogue without being a democrat. In the same way Bernard Shaw is a demagogue without being a democrat. If he had tried to prove his principle from any of the other heroes or sages of mankind he would have found it much more difficult. Napoleon achieved more miraculous conquest; but during his most conquering epoch he was a burning boy suicidally in love with a woman far beyond his age. Joan of Arc achieved far more instant and incredible worldly success; but Joan of Arc achieved worldly success because she believed in another world. Nelson was a figure fully as fascinating and dramatically decisive; but Nelson was "romantic"; Nelson was a devoted patriot and a devoted lover. Alexander was passionate; Cromwell could shed tears; Bismarck had some suburban religion; Frederick was a poet; Charlemagne was fond of children. But Julius Caesar attracted Shaw not less by his positive than by his negative enormousness. Nobody can say with certainty that Caesar cared for anything. It is unjust to call Caesar an egoist; for there is no proof that he cared even for Caesar. He may not have been either an atheist or a pessimist. But he may have been; that is exactly the rub. He may have been an ordinary decently good man slightly deficient in spiritual expansiveness. On the other hand, he may have been the incarnation of paganism in the sense that Christ was the incarnation of Christianity. As Christ expressed how great a man can be humble and humane, Caesar may have expressed how great a man can be frigid and flippant. According to most legends Antichrist was to come soon after Christ. One has only to suppose that Antichrist came shortly before Christ; and Antichrist might very well be Caesar.

It is, I think, no injustice to Bernard Shaw to say that he does not attempt to make his Caesar superior except in this naked and negative sense. There is no suggestion, as there is in the Jehovah of the Old Testament, that the very cruelty of the higher being conceals some tremendous and even tortured love. Caesar is superior to other men not because he loves more, but because he hates less. Caesar is magnanimous not because he is warm-hearted enough to pardon, but because he is not warm-hearted enough to avenge. There is no suggestion anywhere in the play that he is hiding any great genial purpose or powerful tenderness towards men. In order to put this point beyond a doubt the dramatist has introduced a soliloquy of Caesar alone with the Sphinx. There if anywhere he would have broken out into ultimate brotherhood or burning pity for the people. But in that scene between the Sphinx and Caesar, Caesar is as cold and as lonely and as dead as the Sphinx.

But whether the Shavian Caesar is a sound ideal or no, there can be little doubt that he is a very fine reality. Shaw has done nothing greater as a piece of artistic creation. If the man is a little like a statue, it is a statue by a great sculptor; a statue of the best period. If his nobility is a little negative in its character, it is the negative darkness of the great dome of night; not as in some "new moralities" the mere mystery of the coal-hole. Indeed, this somewhat austere method of work is very suitable to Shaw when he is serious. There is nothing Gothic about his real genius; he could not build a mediaeval cathedral in which laughter and terror are twisted together in stone, molten by mystical passion. He can build, by way of amusement, a Chinese pagoda; but when he is in earnest, only a Roman temple. He has a keen eye for truth; but he is one of those people who like, as the saying goes, to put down the truth in black and white. He is always girding and jeering at romantics and idealists because they will not put down the truth in black and white. But black and white are not the only two colours in the world. The modern man of science who writes down a fact in black and white is not more but less accurate than the mediaeval monk who wrote it down in gold and scarlet, sea-green and turquoise. Nevertheless, it is a good thing that the more austere method should exist separately, and that some men should be specially good at it. Bernard Shaw is specially good at it; he is pre-eminently a black and white artist.

And as a study in black and white nothing could be better than this sketch of Julius Caesar. He is not so much represented as "bestriding the earth like a Colossus" (which is indeed a rather comic attitude for a hero to stand in), but rather walking the earth with a sort of stern levity, lightly touching the planet and yet spurning it away like a stone. He walks like a winged man who has chosen to fold his wings. There is something creepy even about his kindness; it makes the men in front of him feel as if they were made of glass. The nature of the Caesarian mercy is massively suggested. Caesar dislikes a massacre, not because it is a great sin, but because it is a small sin. It is felt that he classes it with a flirtation or a fit of the sulks; a senseless temporary subjugation of man's permanent purpose by his passing and trivial feelings. He will plunge into slaughter for a great purpose, just as he plunges into the sea. But to be stung into such action he deems as undignified as to be tipped off the pier. In a singularly fine passage Cleopatra, having hired assassins to stab an enemy, appeals to her wrongs as justifying her revenge, and says, "If you can find one man in all Africa who says that I did wrong, I will be crucified by my own slaves." "If you can find one man in all the world," replies Caesar, "who can see that you did wrong, he will either conquer the world as I have done or be crucified by it." That is the high water mark of this heathen sublimity; and we do not feel it inappropriate, or unlike Shaw, when a few minutes afterwards the hero is saluted with a blaze of swords.

As usually happens in the author's works, there is even more about Julius Caesar in the preface than there is in the play. But in the preface I think the portrait is less imaginative and more fanciful. He attempts to connect his somewhat chilly type of superman with the heroes of the old fairy tales. But Shaw should not talk about the fairy tales; for he does not feel them from the inside. As I have said, on all this side of historic and domestic traditions Bernard Shaw is weak and deficient. He does not approach them as fairy tales, as if he were four, but as "folk-lore" as if he were forty. And he makes a big mistake about them which he would never have made if he had kept his birthday and hung up his stocking, and generally kept alive inside him the firelight of a home. The point is so peculiarly characteristic of Bernard Shaw, and is indeed so much of a summary of his most interesting assertion and his most interesting error, that it deserves a word by itself, though it is a word which must be remembered in connection with nearly all the other plays.

His primary and defiant proposition is the Calvinistic proposition: that the elect do not earn virtue, but possess it. The goodness of a man does not consist in trying to be good, but in being good. Julius Caesar prevails over other people by possessing more virtus than they; not by having striven or suffered or bought his virtue; not because he has struggled heroically, but because he is a hero. So far Bernard Shaw is only what I have called him at the beginning; he is simply a seventeenth-century Calvinist. Caesar is not saved by works, or even by faith; he is saved because he is one of the elect. Unfortunately for himself, however, Bernard Shaw went back further than the seventeenth century; and professing his opinion to be yet more antiquated, invoked the original legends of mankind. He argued that when the fairy tales gave Jack the Giant Killer a coat of darkness or a magic sword it removed all credit from Jack in the "common moral" sense; he won as Caesar won only because he was superior. I will confess, in passing, to the conviction that Bernard Shaw in the course of his whole simple and strenuous life was never quite so near to hell as at the moment when he wrote down those words. But in this question of fairy tales my immediate point is, not how near he was to hell, but how very far off he was from fairyland. That notion about the hero with a magic sword being the superman with a magic superiority is the caprice of a pedant; no child, boy, or man ever felt it in the story of Jack the Giant Killer. Obviously the moral is all the other way. Jack's fairy sword and invisible coat are clumsy expedients for enabling him to fight at all with something which is by nature stronger. They are a rough, savage substitute for psychological descriptions of special valour or unwearied patience. But no one in his five wits can doubt that the idea of "Jack the Giant Killer" is exactly the opposite to Shaw's idea. If it were not a tale of effort and triumph hardly earned it would not be called "Jack the Giant Killer." If it were a tale of the victory of natural advantages it would be called "Giant the Jack Killer." If the teller of fairy tales had merely wanted to urge that some beings are born stronger than others he would not have fallen back on elaborate tricks of weapon and costume for conquering an ogre. He would simply have let the ogre conquer. I will not speak of my own emotions in connection with this incredibly caddish doctrine that the strength of the strong is admirable, but not the valour of the weak. It is enough to say that I have to summon up the physical presence of Shaw, his frank gestures, kind eyes, and exquisite Irish voice, to cure me of a mere sensation of contempt. But I do not dwell upon the point for any such purpose; but merely to show how we must be always casting back to those concrete foundations with which we began. Bernard Shaw, as I have said, was never national enough to be domestic; he was never a part of his past; hence when he tries to interpret tradition he comes a terrible cropper, as in this case. Bernard Shaw (I strongly suspect) began to disbelieve in Santa Claus at a discreditably early age. And by this time Santa Claus has avenged himself by taking away the key of all the prehistoric scriptures; so that a noble and honourable artist flounders about like any German professor. Here is a whole fairy literature which is almost exclusively devoted to the unexpected victory of the weak over the strong; and Bernard Shaw manages to make it mean the inevitable victory of the strong over the weak--which, among other things, would not make a story at all. It all comes of that mistake about not keeping his birthday. A man should be always tied to his mother's apron strings; he should always have a hold on his childhood, and be ready at intervals to start anew from a childish standpoint. Theologically the thing is best expressed by saying, "You must be born again." Secularly it is best expressed by saying, "You must keep your birthday." Even if you will not be born again, at least remind yourself occasionally that you were born once.

Some of the incidental wit in the Caesarian drama is excellent although it is upon the whole less spontaneous and perfect than in the previous plays. One of its jests may be mentioned in passing, not merely to draw attention to its failure (though Shaw is brilliant enough to afford many failures) but because it is the best opportunity for mentioning one of the writer's minor notions to which he obstinately adheres. He describes the Ancient Briton in Caesar's train as being exactly like a modern respectable Englishman. As a joke for a Christmas pantomime this would be all very well; but one expects the jokes of Bernard Shaw to have some intellectual root, however fantastic the flower. And obviously all historic common sense is against the idea that that dim Druid people, whoever they were, who dwelt in our land before it was lit up by Rome or loaded with varied invasions, were a precise facsimile of the commercial society of Birmingham or Brighton. But it is a part of the Puritan in Bernard Shaw, a part of the taut and high-strung quality of his mind, that he will never admit of any of his jokes that it was only a joke. When he has been most witty he will passionately deny his own wit; he will say something which Voltaire might envy and then declare that he has got it all out of a Blue book. And in connection with this eccentric type of self-denial, we may notice this mere detail about the Ancient Briton. Someone faintly hinted that a blue Briton when first found by Caesar might not be quite like Mr. Broadbent; at the touch Shaw poured forth a torrent of theory, explaining that climate was the only thing that affected nationality; and that whatever races came into the English or Irish climate would become like the English or Irish. Now the modern theory of race is certainly a piece of stupid materialism; it is an attempt to explain the things we are sure of, France, Scotland, Rome, Japan, by means of the things we are not sure of at all, prehistoric conjectures, Celts, Mongols, and Iberians. Of course there is a reality in race; but there is no reality in the theories of race offered by some ethnological professors. Blood, perhaps, is thicker than water; but brains are sometimes thicker than anything. But if there is one thing yet more thick and obscure and senseless than this theory of the omnipotence of race it is, I think, that to which Shaw has fled for refuge from it; this doctrine of the omnipotence of climate. Climate again is something; but if climate were everything, Anglo-Indians would grow more and more to look like Hindoos, which is far from being the case. Something in the evil spirit of our time forces people always to pretend to have found some material and mechanical explanation. Bernard Shaw has filled all his last days with affirmations about the divinity of the non-mechanical part of man, the sacred quality in creation and choice. Yet it never seems to have occurred to him that the true key to national differentiations is the key of the will and not of the environment. It never crosses the modern mind to fancy that perhaps a people is chiefly influenced by how that people has chosen to behave. If I have to choose between race and weather I prefer race; I would rather be imprisoned and compelled by ancestors who were once alive than by mud and mists which never were. But I do not propose to be controlled by either; to me my national history is a chain of multitudinous choices. It is neither blood nor rain that has made England, but hope, the thing that all those dead men have desired. France was not France because she was made to be by the skulls of the Celts or by the sun of Gaul. France was France because she chose.

I have stepped on one side from the immediate subject because this is as good an instance as any we are likely to come across of a certain almost extraneous fault which does deface the work of Bernard Shaw. It is a fault only to be mentioned when we have made the solidity of the merits quite clear. To say that Shaw is merely making game of people is demonstrably ridiculous; at least a fairly systematic philosophy can be traced through all his jokes, and one would not insist on such a unity in all the songs of Mr. Dan Leno. I have already pointed out that the genius of Shaw is really too harsh and earnest rather than too merry and irresponsible. I shall have occasion to point out later that Shaw is, in one very serious sense, the very opposite of paradoxical. In any case if any real student of Shaw says that Shaw is only making a fool of him, we can only say that of that student it is very superfluous for anyone to make a fool. But though the dramatist's jests are always serious and generally obvious, he is really affected from time to time by a certain spirit of which that climate theory is a case-- a spirit that can only be called one of senseless ingenuity. I suppose it is a sort of nemesis of wit; the skidding of a wheel in the height of its speed. Perhaps it is connected with the nomadic nature of his mind. That lack of roots, this remoteness from ancient instincts and traditions is responsible for a certain bleak and heartless extravagance of statement on certain subjects which makes the author really unconvincing as well as exaggerative; satires that are saugrenu, jokes that are rather silly than wild, statements which even considered as lies have no symbolic relation to truth. They are exaggerations of something that does not exist. For instance, if a man called Christmas Day a mere hypocritical excuse for drunkenness and gluttony that would be false, but it would have a fact hidden in it somewhere. But when Bernard Shaw says that Christmas Day is only a conspiracy kept up by poulterers and wine merchants from strictly business motives, then he says something which is not so much false as startlingly and arrestingly foolish. He might as well say that the two sexes were invented by jewellers who wanted to sell wedding rings. Or again, take the case of nationality and the unit of patriotism. If a man said that all boundaries between clans, kingdoms, or empires were nonsensical or non-existent, that would be a fallacy, but a consistent and philosophical fallacy. But when Mr. Bernard Shaw says that England matters so little that the British Empire might very well give up these islands to Germany, he has not only got hold of the sow by the wrong ear but the wrong sow by the wrong ear; a mythical sow, a sow that is not there at all. If Britain is unreal, the British Empire must be a thousand times more unreal. It is as if one said, "I do not believe that Michael Scott ever had any existence; but I am convinced, in spite of the absurd legend, that he had a shadow."

As has been said already, there must be some truth in every popular impression. And the impression that Shaw, the most savagely serious man of his time, is a mere music-hall artist must have reference to such rare outbreaks as these. As a rule his speeches are full, not only of substance, but of substances, materials like pork, mahogany, lead, and leather. There is no man whose arguments cover a more Napoleonic map of detail. It is true that he jokes; but wherever he is he has topical jokes, one might almost say family jokes. If he talks to tailors he can allude to the last absurdity about buttons. If he talks to the soldiers he can see the exquisite and exact humour of the last gun-carriage. But when all his powerful practicality is allowed, there does run through him this erratic levity, an explosion of ineptitude. It is a queer quality in literature. It is a sort of cold extravagance; and it has made him all his enemies.

* * * *

The Philosopher

I SHOULD suppose that Caesar and Cleopatra marks about the turning tide of Bernard Shaw's fortune and fame. Up to this time he had known glory, but never success. He had been wondered at as something brilliant and barren, like a meteor; but no one would accept him as a sun, for the test of a sun is that it can make something grow. Practically speaking the two qualities of a modern drama are, that it should play and that it should pay. It had been proved over and over again in weighty dramatic criticisms, in careful readers' reports, that the plays of Shaw could never play or pay; that the public did not want wit and the wars of intellect. And just about the time that this had been finally proved, the plays of Bernard Shaw promised to play like Charley's Aunt and to pay like Colman's Mustard. It is a fact in which we can all rejoice, not only because it redeems the reputation of Bernard Shaw, but because it redeems the character of the English people. All that is bravest in human nature, open challenge and unexpected wit and angry conviction, are not so very unpopular as the publishers and managers in their motor-cars have been in the habit of telling us. But exactly because we have come to a turning point in the man's career I propose to interrupt the mere catalogue of his plays and to treat his latest series rather as the proclamations of an acknowledged prophet. For the last plays, especially Man and Superman, are such that his whole position must be re-stated before attacking them seriously.

For two reasons I have called this concluding series of plays not again by the name of "The Dramatist," but by the general name of "The Philosopher." The first reason is that given above, that we have come to the time of his triumph and may therefore treat him as having gained complete possession of a pulpit of his own. But there is a second reason: that it was just about this time that he began to create not only a pulpit of his own, but a church and creed of his own. It is a very vast and universal religion; and it is not his fault that he is the only member of it. The plainer way of putting it is this: that here, in the hour of his earthly victory, there dies in him the old mere denier, the mere dynamiter of criticism. In the warmth of popularity he begins to wish to put his faith positively; to offer some solid key to all creation. Perhaps the irony in the situation is this: that all the crowds are acclaiming him as the blasting and hypercritical buffoon, while he himself is seriously rallying his synthetic power, and with a grave face telling himself that it is time he had a faith to preach. His final success as a sort of charlatan coincides with his first grand failures as a theologian.

For this reason I have deliberately called a halt in his dramatic career, in order to consider these two essential points: What did the mass of Englishmen, who had now learnt to admire him, imagine his point of view to be? and second, What did he imagine it to be? or, if the phrase be premature, What did he imagine it was going to be? In his latest work, especially in _Man and Superman,_ Shaw has become a complete and colossal mystic. That mysticism does grow quite rationally out of his older arguments; but very few people ever troubled to trace the connection. In order to do so it is necessary to say what was, at the time of his first success, the public impression of Shaw's philosophy.

Now it is an irritating and pathetic thing that the three most popular phrases about Shaw are false. Modern criticism, like all weak things, is overloaded with words. In a healthy condition of language a man finds it very difficult to say the right thing, but at last says it. In this empire of journalese a man finds it so very easy to say the wrong thing that he never thinks of saying anything else. False or meaningless phrases lie so ready to his hand that it is easier to use them than not to use them. These wrong terms picked up through idleness are retained through habit, and so the man has begun to think wrong almost before he has begun to think at all. Such lumbering logomachy is always injurious and oppressive to men of spirit, imagination or intellectual honour, and it has dealt very recklessly and wrongly with Bernard Shaw. He has contrived to get about three newspaper phrases tied to his tail; and those newspaper phrases are all and separately wrong. The three superstitions about him, it will be conceded, are generally these: first that he desires "problem plays," second that he is "paradoxical," and third that in his dramas as elsewhere he is specially "a Socialist." And the interesting thing is that when we come to his philosophy, all these three phrases are quite peculiarly inapplicable.

To take the plays first, there is a general disposition to describe that type of intimate or defiant drama which he approves as "the problem play." Now the serious modern play is, as a rule, the very reverse of a problem play; for there can be no problem unless both points of view are equally and urgently presented. Hamlet really is a problem play because at the end of it one is really in doubt as to whether upon the author's showing Hamlet is something more than a man or something less. Henry IV and Henry V are really problem plays; in this sense, that the reader or spectator is really doubtful whether the high but harsh efficiency, valour, and ambition of Henry V are an improvement on his old blackguard camaraderie; and whether he was not a better man when he was a thief. This hearty and healthy doubt is very common in Shakespeare; I mean a doubt that exists in the writer as well as in the reader. But Bernard Shaw is far too much of a Puritan to tolerate such doubts about points which he counts essential. There is no sort of doubt that the young lady in Arms and the Man is improved by losing her ideals. There is no sort of doubt that Captain Brassbound is improved by giving up the object of his life. But a better case can be found in something that both dramatists have been concerned with; Shaw wrote Caesar and Cleopatra; Shakespeare wrote Antony and Cleopatra and also Julius Caesar. And exactly what annoys Bernard Shaw about Shakespeare's version is this: that Shakespeare has an open mind or, in other words, that Shakespeare has really written a problem play. Shakespeare sees quite as clearly as Shaw that Brutus is unpractical and ineffectual; but he also sees, what is quite as plain and practical a fact, that these ineffectual men do capture the hearts and influence the policies of mankind. Shaw would have nothing said in favour of Brutus; because Brutus is on the wrong side in politics. Of the actual problem of public and private morality, as it was presented to Brutus, he takes actually no notice at all. He can write the most energetic and outspoken of propaganda plays; but he cannot rise to a problem play. He cannot really divide his mind and let the two parts speak independently to each other. He has never, so to speak, actually split his head in two; though I daresay there are many other people who are willing to do it for him.

Sometimes, especially in his later plays, he allows his clear conviction to spoil even his admirable dialogue, making one side entirely weak, as in an Evangelical tract. I do not know whether in Major Barbara the young Greek professor was supposed to be a fool. As popular tradition (which I trust more than anything else) declared that he is drawn from a real Professor of my acquaintance, who is anything but a fool, I should imagine not. But in that case I am all the more mystified by the incredibly weak fight which he makes in the play in answer to the elephantine sophistries of Undershaft. It is really a disgraceful case, and almost the only case in Shaw of there being no fair fight between the two sides. For instance, the Professor mentions pity. Mr. Undershaft says with melodramatic scorn, "Pity! the scavenger of the Universe!" Now if any gentleman had said this to me, I should have replied, "If I permit you to escape from the point by means of metaphors, will you tell me whether you disapprove of scavengers?" Instead of this obvious retort, the miserable Greek professor only says, "Well then, love," to which Undershaft replies with unnecessary violence that he won't have the Greek professor's love, to which the obvious answer of course would be, "How the deuce can you prevent my loving you if I choose to do so?" Instead of this, as far as I remember, that abject Hellenist says nothing at all. I only mention this unfair dialogue, because it marks, I think, the recent hardening, for good or evil, of Shaw out of a dramatist into a mere philosopher, and whoever hardens into a philosopher may be hardening into a fanatic.

And just as there is nothing really problematic in Shaw's mind, so there is nothing really paradoxical. The meaning of the word paradoxical may indeed be made the subject of argument. In Greek, of course, it simply means something which is against the received opinion; in that sense a missionary remonstrating with South Sea cannibals is paradoxical. But in the much more important world, where words are used and altered in the using, paradox does not mean merely this: it means at least something of which the antinomy or apparent inconsistency is sufficiently plain in the words used, and most commonly of all it means an idea expressed in a form which is verbally contradictory. Thus, for instance, the great saying, "He that shall lose his life, the same shall save it," is an example of what modern people mean by a paradox. If any learned person should read this book (which seems immeasurably improbable) he can content himself with putting it this way, that the moderns mistakenly say paradox when they should say oxymoron. Ultimately, in any case, it may be agreed that we commonly mean by a paradox some kind of collision between what is seemingly and what is really true.

Now if by paradox we mean truth inherent in a contradiction, as in the saying of Christ that I have quoted, it is a very curious fact that Bernard Shaw is almost entirely without paradox. Moreover, he cannot even understand a paradox. And more than this, paradox is about the only thing in the world that he does not understand. All his splendid vistas and startling suggestions arise from carrying some one clear principle further than it has yet been carried. His madness is all consistency, not inconsistency. As the point can hardly be made clear without examples, let us take one example, the subject of education. Shaw has been all his life preaching to grownup people the profound truth that liberty and responsibility go together; that the reason why freedom is so often easily withheld, is simply that it is a terrible nuisance. This is true, though not the whole truth, of citizens; and so when Shaw comes to children he can only apply to them the same principle that he has already applied to citizens. He begins to play with the Herbert Spencer idea of teaching children by experience; perhaps the most fatuously silly idea that was ever gravely put down in print. On that there is no need to dwell; one has only to ask how the experimental method is to be applied to a precipice; and the theory no longer exists. But Shaw effected a further development, if possible more fantastic. He said that one should never tell a child anything without letting him hear the opposite opinion. That is to say, when you tell Tommy not to hit his sick sister on the temple, you must make sure of the presence of some Nietzscheite professor, who will explain to him that such a course might possibly serve to eliminate the unfit. When you are in the act of telling Susan not to drink out of the bottle labelled "poison," you must telegraph for a Christian Scientist, who will be ready to maintain that without her own consent it cannot do her any harm. What would happen to a child brought up on Shaw's principle I cannot conceive; I should think he would commit suicide in his bath. But that is not here the question. The point is that this proposition seems quite sufficiently wild and startling to ensure that its author, if he escapes Hanwell, would reach the front rank of journalists, demagogues, or public entertainers. It is a perfect paradox, if a paradox only means something that makes one jump. But it is not a paradox at all in the sense of a contradiction. It is not a contradiction, but an enormous and outrageous consistency, the one principle of free thought carried to a point to which no other sane man would consent to carry it. Exactly what Shaw does not understand is the paradox; the unavoidable paradox of childhood. Although this child is much better than I, yet I must teach it. Although this being has much purer passions than I, yet I must control it. Although Tommy is quite right to rush towards a precipice, yet he must be stood in the corner for doing it. This contradiction is the only possible condition of having to do with children at all; anyone who talks about a child without feeling this paradox might just as well be talking about a merman. He has never even seen the animal. But this paradox Shaw in his intellectual simplicity cannot see; he cannot see it because it is a paradox. His only intellectual excitement is to carry one idea further and further across the world. It never occurs to him that it might meet another idea, and like the three winds in Martin Chuzzlewit, they might make a night of it. His only paradox is to pull out one thread or cord of truth longer and longer into waste and fantastic places. He does not allow for that deeper sort of paradox by which two opposite cords of truth become entangled in an inextricable knot. Still less can he be made to realise that it is often this knot which ties safely together the whole bundle of human life.

This blindness to paradox everywhere perplexes his outlook. He cannot understand marriage because he will not understand the paradox of marriage; that the woman is all the more the house for not being the head of it. He cannot understand patriotism, because he will not understand the paradox of patriotism; that one is all the more human for not merely loving humanity. He does not understand Christianity because he will not understand the paradox of

Christianity; that we can only really understand all myths when we know that one of them is true. I do not under-rate him for this anti-paradoxical temper; I concede that much of his finest and keenest work in the way of intellectual purification would have been difficult or impossible without it. But I say that here lies the limitation of that lucid and compelling mind; he cannot quite understand life, because he will not accept its contradictions.

Nor is it by any means descriptive of Shaw to call him a Socialist; in so far as that word can be extended to cover an ethical attitude. He is the least social of all Socialists; and I pity the Socialist state that tries to manage him. This anarchism of his is not a question of thinking for himself; every decent man thinks for himself; it would be highly immodest to think for anybody else. Nor is it any instinctive licence or egoism; as I have said before, he is a man of peculiarly acute public conscience. The unmanageable part of him, the fact that he cannot be conceived as part of a crowd or as really and invisibly helping a movement, has reference to another thing in him, or rather to another thing not in him.

The great defect of that fine intelligence is a failure to grasp and enjoy the things commonly called convention and tradition; which are foods upon which all human creatures must feed frequently if they are to live. Very few modern people of course have any idea of what they are. "Convention" is very nearly the same word as "democracy." It has again and again in history been used as an alternative word to Parliament. So far from suggesting anything stale or sober, the word convention rather conveys a hubbub; it is the coming together of men; every mob is a convention. In its secondary sense it means the common soul of such a crowd, its instinctive anger at the traitor or its instinctive salutation of the flag. Conventions may be cruel, they may be unsuitable, they may even be grossly superstitious or obscene; but there is one thing that they never are. Conventions are never dead. They are always full of accumulated emotions, the piled-up and passionate experiences of many generations asserting what they could not explain. To be inside any true convention, as the Chinese respect for parents or the European respect for children, is to be surrounded by something which whatever else it is is not leaden, lifeless or automatic, something which is taut and tingling with vitality at a hundred points, which is sensitive almost to madness and which is so much alive that it can kill. Now Bernard Shaw has always made this one immense mistake (arising out of that bad progressive education of his), the mistake of treating convention as a dead thing; treating it as if it were a mere physical environment like the pavement or the rain. Whereas it is a result of will; a rain of blessings and a pavement of good intentions. Let it be remembered that I am not discussing in what degree one should allow for tradition; I am saying that men like Shaw do not allow for it at all. If Shaw had found in early life that he was contradicted by Bradshaw's Railway Guide or even by the Encyclopaedia Britannica, he would have felt at least that he might be wrong. But if he had found himself contradicted by his father and mother, he would have thought it all the more probable that he was right. If the issue of the last evening paper contradicted him he might be troubled to investigate or explain. That the human tradition of two thousand years contradicted him did not trouble him for an instant. That Marx was not with him was important. That Man was not with him was an irrelevant prehistoric joke. People have talked far too much about the paradoxes of Bernard Shaw. Perhaps his only pure paradox is this almost unconscious one; that he has tended to think that because something has satisfied generations of men it must be untrue.

Shaw is wrong about nearly all the things one learns early in life and while one is still simple. Most human beings start with certain facts of psychology to which the rest of life must be somewhat related. For instance, every man falls in love; and no man falls into free love. When he falls into that he calls it lust, and is always ashamed of it even when he boasts of it. That there is some connection between a love and a vow nearly every human being knows before he is eighteen. That there is a solid and instinctive connection between the idea of sexual ecstasy and the idea of some sort of almost suicidal constancy, this I say is simply the first fact in one's own psychology; boys and girls know it almost before they know their own language. How far it can be trusted, how it can best be dealt with, all that is another matter. But lovers lust after constancy more than after happiness; if you are in any sense prepared to give them what they ask, then what they ask, beyond all question, is an oath of final fidelity. Lovers may be lunatics; lovers may be children; lovers may be unfit for citizenship and outside human argument; you can take up that position if you will. But lovers do not only desire love; they desire marriage. The root of legal monogamy does not lie (as Shaw and his friends are for ever drearily asserting) in the fact that the man is a mere tyrant and the woman a mere slave. It lies in the fact that if their love for each other is the noblest and freest love conceivable, it can only find its heroic expression in both becoming slaves. I only mention this matter here as a matter which most of us do not need to be taught; for it was the first lesson of life. In after years we may make up what code or compromise about sex we like; but we all know that constancy, jealousy, and the personal pledge are natural and inevitable in sex; we do not feel any surprise when we see them either in a murder or in a valentine. We may or may not see wisdom in early marriages; but we know quite well that wherever the thing is genuine at all, early loves will mean early marriages. But Shaw had not learnt about this tragedy of the sexes, what the rustic ballads of any country on earth would have taught him. He had not learnt, what universal common sense has put into all the folk-lore of the earth, that love cannot be thought of clearly for an instant except as monogamous. The old English ballads never sing the praises of "lovers." They always sing the praises of "true lovers," and that is the final philosophy of the question.

The same is true of Mr. Shaw's refusal to understand the love of the land either in the form of patriotism or of private ownership. It is the attitude of an Irishman cut off from the soil of Ireland, retaining the audacity and even cynicism of the national type, but no longer fed from the roots with its pathos or its experience.

This broader and more brotherly rendering of convention must be applied particularly to the conventions of the drama; since that is necessarily the most democratic of all the arts. And it will be found generally that most of the theatrical conventions rest on a real artistic basis. The Greek Unities, for instance, were not proper objects of the meticulous and trivial imitation of Seneca or Gabriel Harvey. But still less were they the right objects for the equally trivial and far more vulgar impatience of men like Macaulay. That a tale should, if possible, be told of one place or one day or a manageable number of characters is an ideal plainly rooted in an aesthetic instinct. But if this be so with the classical drama, it is yet more certainly so with romantic drama, against the somewhat decayed dignity of which Bernard Shaw was largely in rebellion. There was one point in particular upon which the Ibsenites claimed to have reformed the romantic convention which is worthy of special allusion.

Shaw and all the other Ibsenites were fond of insisting that a defect in the romantic drama was its tendency to end with wedding-bells. Against this they set the modern drama of middle-age, the drama which described marriage itself instead of its poetic preliminaries. Now if Bernard Shaw had been more patient with popular tradition, more prone to think that there might be some sense in its survival, he might have seen this particular problem much more clearly. The old playwrights have left us plenty of plays of marriage and middle-age. Othello is as much about what follows the wedding-bells as The Doll's House. Macbeth is about a middle-aged couple as much as Little Eyolf. But if we ask ourselves what is the real difference, we shall, I think, find that it can fairly be stated thus. The old tragedies of marriage, though not love stories, are like love stories in this, that they work up to some act or stroke which is irrevocable as marriage is irrevocable; to the fact of death or of adultery.

Now the reason why our fathers did not make marriage, in the middle-aged and static sense, the subject of their plays was a very simple one; it was that a play is a very bad place for discussing that topic. You cannot easily make a good drama out of the success or failure of a marriage, just as you could not make a good drama out of the growth of an oak tree or the decay of an empire. As Polonius very reasonably observed, it is too long. A happy love-affair will make a drama simply because it is dramatic; it depends on an ultimate yes or no. But a happy marriage is not dramatic; perhaps it would be less happy if it were. The essence of a romantic heroine is that she asks herself an intense question; but the essence of a sensible wife is that she is much too sensible to ask herself any questions at all. All the things that make monogamy a success are in their nature undramatic things, the silent growth of an instinctive confidence, the common wounds and victories, the accumulation of customs, the rich maturing of old jokes. Sane marriage is an untheatrical thing; it is therefore not surprising that most modern dramatists have devoted themselves to insane marriage.

To summarise; before touching the philosophy which Shaw has ultimately adopted, we must quit the notion that we know it already and that it is hit off in such journalistic terms as these three. Shaw does not wish to multiply problem plays or even problems. He has such scepticism as is the misfortune of his age; but he has this dignified and courageous quality, that he does not come to ask questions but to answer them. He is not a paradox-monger; he is a wild logician, far too simple even to be called a sophist. He understands everything in life except its paradoxes, especially that ultimate paradox that the very things that we cannot comprehend are the things that we have to take for granted. Lastly, he is not especially social or collectivist. On the contrary, he rather dislikes men in the mass, though he can appreciate them individually.

He has no respect for collective humanity in its two great forms; either in that momentary form which we call a mob, or in that enduring form which we call a convention.

The general cosmic theory which can so far be traced through the earlier essays and plays of Bernard Shaw may be expressed in the image of Schopenhauer standing on his head. I cheerfully concede that Schopenhauer looks much nicer in that posture than in his original one, but I can hardly suppose that he feels more comfortable. The substance of the change is this. Roughly speaking, Schopenhauer maintained that life is unreasonable. The intellect, if it could be impartial, would tell us to cease; but a blind partiality, an instinct quite distinct from thought, drives us on to take desperate chances in an essentially bankrupt lottery. Shaw seems to accept this dingy estimate of the rational outlook, but adds a somewhat arresting comment. Schopenhauer had said, "Life is unreasonable; so much the worse for all living things." Shaw said, "Life is unreasonable; so much the worse for reason." Life is the higher call, life we must follow. It may be that there is some undetected fallacy in reason itself. Perhaps the whole man cannot get inside his own head any more than he can jump down his own throat. But there is about the need to live, to suffer, and to create that imperative quality which can truly be called supernatural, of whose voice it can indeed be said that it speaks with authority, and not as the scribes.

This is the first and finest item of the original Bernard Shaw creed: that if reason says that life is irrational, life must be content to reply that reason is lifeless; life is the primary thing, and if reason impedes it, then reason must be trodden down into the mire amid the most abject superstitions. In the ordinary sense it would be specially absurd to suggest that Shaw desires man to be a mere animal. For that is always associated with lust or incontinence; and Shaw's ideals are strict, hygienic, and even, one might say, old-maidish. But there is a mystical sense in which one may say literally that Shaw desires man to be an animal. That is, he desires him to cling first and last to life, to the spirit of animation, to the thing which is common to him and the birds and plants. Man should have the blind faith of a beast: he should be as mystically immutable as a cow, and as deaf to sophistries as a fish. Shaw does not wish him to be a philosopher or an artist; he does not even wish him to be a man, so much as he wishes him to be, in this holy sense, an animal. He must follow the flag of life as fiercely from conviction as all other creatures follow it from instinct.

But this Shavian worship of life is by no means lively. It has nothing in common either with the braver or the baser forms of what we commonly call optimism. It has none of the omnivorous exultation of Walt Whitman or the fiery pantheism of Shelley. Bernard Shaw wishes to show himself not so much as an optimist, but rather as a sort of faithful and contented pessimist. This contradiction is the key to nearly all his early and more obvious contradictions and to many which remain to the end. Whitman and many modern idealists have talked of taking even duty as a pleasure; it seems to me that Shaw takes even pleasure as a duty. In a queer way he seems to see existence as an illusion and yet as an obligation. To every man and woman, bird, beast, and flower, life is a love-call to be eagerly followed. To Bernard Shaw it is merely a military bugle to be obeyed. In short, he fails to feel that the command of Nature (if one must use the anthropomorphic fable of Nature instead of the philosophic term God) can be enjoyed as well as obeyed. He paints life at its darkest and then tells the babe unborn to take the leap in the dark. That is heroic; and to my instinct at least Schopenhauer looks like a pigmy beside his pupil. But it is the heroism of a morbid and almost asphyxiated age. It is awful to think that this world which so many poets have praised has even for a time been depicted as a man-trap into which we may just have the manhood to jump. Think of all those ages through which men have talked of having the courage to die. And then remember that we have actually fallen to talking about having the courage to live.

It is exactly this oddity or dilemma which may be said to culminate in the crowning work of his later and more constructive period, the work in which he certainly attempted, whether with success or not, to state his ultimate and cosmic vision; I mean the play called Man and Superman. In approaching this play we must keep well in mind the distinction recently drawn: that Shaw follows the banner of life, but austerely, not joyously. For him nature has authority, but hardly charm. But before we approach it it is necessary to deal with three things that lead up to it. First it is necessary to speak of what remained of his old critical and realistic method; and then it is necessary to speak of the two important influences which led up to his last and most important change of outlook.

First, since all our spiritual epochs overlap, and a man is often doing the old work while he is thinking of the new, we may deal first with what may be fairly called his last two plays of pure worldly criticism. These are Major Barbara and John Bull's Other Island. Major Barbara indeed contains a strong religious element; but, when all is said, the whole point of the play is that the religious element is defeated. Moreover, the actual expressions of religion in the play are somewhat unsatisfactory as expressions of religion--or even of reason. I must frankly say that Bernard Shaw always seems to me to use the word God not only without any idea of what it means, but without one moment's thought about what it could possibly mean. He said to some atheist, "Never believe in a God that you cannot improve on." The atheist (being a sound theologian) naturally replied that one should not believe in a God whom one could improve on; as that would show that he was not God. In the same style in Major Barbara the heroine ends by suggesting that she will serve God without personal hope, so that she may owe nothing to God and He owe everything to her. It does not seem to strike her that if God owes everything to her He is not God. These things affect me merely as tedious perversions of a phrase. It is as if you said, "I will never have a father unless I have begotten him."

But the real sting and substance of Major Barbara is much more practical and to the point. It expresses not the new spirituality but the old materialism of Bernard Shaw. Almost every one of Shaw's plays is an expanded epigram. But the epigram is not expanded (as with most people) into a hundred commonplaces. Rather the epigram is expanded into a hundred other epigrams; the work is at least as brilliant in detail as it is in design. But it is generally possible to discover the original and pivotal epigram which is the centre and purpose of the play. It is generally possible, even amid that blinding jewellery of a million jokes, to discover the grave, solemn and sacred joke for which the play itself was written.

The ultimate epigram of Major Barbara can be put thus. People say that poverty is no crime; Shaw says that poverty is a crime; that it is a crime to endure it, a crime to be content with it, that it is the mother of all crimes of brutality, corruption, and fear. If a man says to Shaw that he is born of poor but honest parents, Shaw tells him that the very word "but" shows that his parents were probably dishonest. In short, he maintains here what he had maintained elsewhere: that what the people at this moment require is not more patriotism or more art or more religion or more morality or more sociology, but simply more money. The evil is not ignorance or decadence or sin or pessimism; the evil is poverty. The point of this particular drama is that even the noblest enthusiasm of the girl who becomes a Salvation Army officer fails under the brute money power of her father who is a modern capitalist. When I have said this it will be clear why this play, fine and full of bitter sincerity as it is, must in a manner be cleared out of the way before we come to talk of Shaw's final and serious faith. For his serious faith is in the sanctity of human will, in the divine capacity for creation and choice rising higher than environment and doom; and so far as that goes, Major Barbara is not only apart from his faith but against his faith. Major Barbara is an account of environment victorious over heroic will. There are a thousand answers to the ethic in Major Barbara which I should be inclined to offer. I might point out that the rich do not so much buy honesty as curtains to cover dishonesty: that they do not so much buy health as cushions to comfort disease. And I might suggest that the doctrine that poverty degrades the poor is much more likely to be used as an argument for keeping them powerless than as an argument for making them rich. But there is no need to find such answers to the materialistic pessimism of Major Barbara. The best answer to it is in Shaw's own best and crowning philosophy, with which we shall shortly be concerned.

John Bull's Other Island represents a realism somewhat more tinged with the later transcendentalism of its author. In one sense, of course, it is a satire on the conventional Englishman, who is never so silly or sentimental as when he sees silliness and sentiment in the Irishman. Broadbent, whose mind is all fog and his morals all gush, is firmly persuaded that he is bringing reason and order among the Irish, whereas in truth they are all smiling at his illusions with the critical detachment of so many devils. There have been many plays depicting the absurd Paddy in a ring of Anglo-Saxons; the first purpose of this play is to depict the absurd Anglo-Saxon in a ring of ironical Paddies. But it has a second and more subtle purpose, which is very finely contrived. It is suggested that when all is said and done there is in this preposterous Englishman a certain creative power which comes from his simplicity and optimism, from his profound resolution rather to live life than to criticise it. I know no finer dialogue of philosophical cross-purposes than that in which Broadbent boasts of his common-sense, and his subtler Irish friend mystifies him by telling him that he, Broadbent, has no common-sense, but only inspiration. The Irishman admits in Broadbent a certain unconscious spiritual force even in his very stupidity. Lord Rosebery coined the very clever phrase "a practical mystic." Shaw is here maintaining that all practical men are practical mystics. And he is really maintaining also that the most practical of all the practical mystics is the one who is a fool.

There is something unexpected and fascinating about this reversal of the usual argument touching enterprise and the business man; this theory that success is created not by intelligence, but by a certain half-witted and yet magical instinct. For Bernard Shaw, apparently, the forests of factories and the mountains of money are not the creations of human wisdom or even of human cunning; they are rather manifestations of the sacred maxim which declares that God has chosen the foolish things of the earth to confound the wise. It is simplicity and even innocence that has made Manchester. As a philosophical fancy this is interesting or even suggestive; but it must be confessed that as a criticism of the relations of England to Ireland it is open to a strong historical objection. The one weak point in John Bull's Other Island is that it turns on the fact that Broadbent succeeds in Ireland. But as a matter of fact Broadbent has not succeeded in Ireland. If getting what one wants is the test and fruit of this mysterious strength, then the Irish peasants are certainly much stronger than the English merchants; for in spite of all the efforts of the merchants, the land has remained a land of peasants. No glorification of the English practicality as if it were a universal thing can ever get over the fact that we have failed in dealing with the one white people in our power who were markedly unlike ourselves. And the kindness of Broadbent has failed just as much as his common-sense; because he was dealing with a people whose desire and ideal were different from his own. He did not share the Irish passion for small possession in land or for the more pathetic virtues of Christianity. In fact the kindness of Broadbent has failed for the same reason that the gigantic kindness of Shaw has failed. The roots are different; it is like tying the tops of two trees together. Briefly, the philosophy of John Bull's Other Island is quite effective and satisfactory except for this incurable fault: the fact that John Bull's other island is not John Bull's.

This clearing off of his last critical plays we may classify as the first of the three facts which lead up to Man and Superman. The second of the three facts may be found, I think, in Shaw's discovery of Nietzsche. This eloquent sophist has an influence upon Shaw and his school which it would require a separate book adequately to study. By descent Nietzsche was a Pole, and probably a Polish noble; and to say that he was a Polish noble is to say that he was a frail, fastidious, and entirely useless anarchist. He had a wonderful poetic wit; and is one of the best rhetoricians of the modern world. He had a remarkable power of saying things that master the reason for a moment by their gigantic unreasonableness; as, for instance, "Your life is intolerable without immortality; but why should not your life be intolerable?" His whole work is shot through with the pangs and fevers of his physical life, which was one of extreme bad health; and in early middle age his brilliant brain broke down into impotence and darkness. All that was true in his teaching was this: that if a man looks fine on a horse it is so far irrelevant to tell him that he would be more economical on a donkey or more humane on a tricycle. In other words, the mere achievement of dignity, beauty, or triumph is strictly to be called a good thing. I do not know if Nietzsche ever used the illustration; but it seems to me that all that is creditable or sound in Nietzsche could be stated in the derivation of one word, the word "valour." Valour means valeur; it means a value; courage is itself a solid good; it is an ultimate virtue; valour is in itself valid. In so far as he maintained this Nietzsche was only taking part in that great Protestant game of see-saw which has been the amusement of northern Europe since the sixteenth century. Nietzsche imagined he was rebelling against ancient morality; as a matter of fact he was only rebelling against recent morality, against the half-baked impudence of the utilitarians and the materialists. He thought he was rebelling against Christianity; curiously enough he was rebelling solely against the special enemies of Christianity, against Herbert Spencer and Mr. Edward Clodd. Historic Christianity has always believed in the valour of St. Michael riding in front of the Church Militant; and in an ultimate and absolute pleasure, not indirect or utilitarian, the intoxication of the spirit, the wine of the blood of God.

There are indeed doctrines of Nietzsche that are not Christian, but then, by an entertaining coincidence, they are also not true. His hatred of pity is not Christian, but that was not his doctrine but his disease. Invalids are often hard on invalids. And there is another doctrine of his that is not Christianity, and also (by the same laughable accident) not common-sense; and it is a most pathetic circumstance that this was the one doctrine which caught the eye of Shaw and captured him. He was not influenced at all by the morbid attack on mercy. It would require more than ten thousand mad Polish professors to make Bernard Shaw anything but a generous and compassionate man. But it is certainly a nuisance that the one Nietzsche doctrine which attracted him was not the one Nietzsche doctrine that is human and rectifying. Nietzsche might really have done some good if he had taught Bernard Shaw to draw the sword, to drink wine, or even to dance. But he only succeeded in putting into his head a new superstition, which bids fair to be the chief superstition of the dark ages which are possibly in front of us--I mean the superstition of what is called the Superman.

In one of his least convincing phrases, Nietzsche had said that just as the ape ultimately produced the man, so should we ultimately produce something higher than the man. The immediate answer, of course, is sufficiently obvious: the ape did not worry about the man, so why should we worry about the Superman? If the Superman will come by natural selection, may we leave it to natural selection? If the Superman will come by human selection, what sort of Superman are we to select? If he is simply to be more just, more brave, or more merciful, then Zarathustra sinks into a Sunday-school teacher; the only way we can work for it is to be more just, more brave, and more merciful; sensible advice, but hardly startling. If he is to be anything else than this, why should we desire him, or what else are we to desire? These questions have been many times asked of the Nietzscheites, and none of the Nietzscheites have even attempted to answer them.

The keen intellect of Bernard Shaw would, I think, certainly have seen through this fallacy and verbiage had it not been that another important event about this time came to the help of Nietzsche and established the Superman on his pedestal. It is the third of the things which I have called stepping-stones to Man and Superman, and it is very important. It is nothing less than the break-down of one of the three intellectual supports upon which Bernard Shaw had reposed through all his confident career. At the beginning of this book I have described the three ultimate supports of Shaw as the Irishman, the Puritan, and the Progressive. They are the three legs of the tripod upon which the prophet sat to give the oracle; and one of them broke. Just about this time suddenly, by a mere shaft of illumination, Bernard Shaw ceased to believe in progress altogether.

It is generally implied that it was reading Plato that did it. That philosopher was very well qualified to convey the first shock of the ancient civilisation to Shaw, who had always thought instinctively of civilisation as modern. This is not due merely to the daring splendour of the speculations and the vivid picture of Athenian life, it is due also to something analogous in the personalities of that particular ancient Greek and this particular modern Irishman. Bernard Shaw has much affinity to Plato--in his instinctive elevation of temper, his courageous pursuit of ideas as far as they will go, his civic idealism; and also, it must be confessed, in his dislike of poets and a touch of delicate inhumanity. But whatever influence produced the change, the change had all the dramatic suddenness and completeness which belongs to the conversions of great men. It had been perpetually implied through all the earlier works not only that mankind is constantly improving, but that almost everything must be considered in the light of this fact. More than once he seemed to argue, in comparing the dramatists of the sixteenth with those of the nineteenth century, that the latter had a definite advantage merely because they were of the nineteenth century and not of the sixteenth. When accused of impertinence towards the greatest of the Elizabethans, Bernard Shaw had said, "Shakespeare is a much taller man than I. but I stand on his shoulders"-- an epigram which sums up this doctrine with characteristic neatness. But Shaw fell off Shakespeare's shoulders with a crash. This chronological theory that Shaw stood on Shakespeare's shoulders logically involved the supposition that Shakespeare stood on Plato's shoulders. And Bernard Shaw found Plato from his point of view so much more advanced than Shakespeare that he decided in desperation that all three were equal.

Such failure as has partially attended the idea of human equality is very largely due to the fact that no party in the modern state has heartily believed in it. Tories and Radicals have both assumed that one set of men were in essentials superior to mankind. The only difference was that the Tory superiority was a superiority of place; while the Radical superiority is a superiority of time. The great objection to Shaw being on Shakespeare's shoulders is a consideration for the sensations and personal dignity of Shakespeare. It is a democratic objection to anyone being on anyone else's shoulders. Eternal human nature refuses to submit to a man who rules merely by right of birth. To rule by right of century is to rule by right of birth. Shaw found his nearest kinsman in remote Athens, his remotest enemies in the closest historical proximity; and he began to see the enormous average and the vast level of mankind. If progress swung constantly between such extremes it could not be progress at all. The paradox was sharp but undeniable; if life had such continual ups and downs, it was upon the whole flat. With characteristic sincerity and love of sensation he had no sooner seen this than he hastened to declare it. In the teeth of all his previous pronouncements he emphasised and re-emphasised in print that man had not progressed at all; that ninety-nine hundredths of a man in a cave were the same as ninety-nine hundredths of a man in a suburban villa.

It is characteristic of him to say that he rushed into print with a frank confession of the failure of his old theory. But it is also characteristic of him that he rushed into print also with a new alternative theory, quite as definite, quite as confident, and, if one may put it so, quite as infallible as the old one. Progress had never happened hitherto, because it had been sought solely through education. Education was rubbish. "Fancy," said he, "trying to produce a greyhound or a racehorse by education!" The man of the future must not be taught; he must be bred. This notion of producing superior human beings by the methods of the stud-farm had often been urged, though its difficulties had never been cleared up. I mean its practical difficulties; its moral difficulties, or rather impossibilities, for any animal fit to be called a man need scarcely be discussed. But even as a scheme it had never been made clear. The first and most obvious objection to it of course is this: that if you are to breed men as pigs, you require some overseer who is as much more subtle than a man as a man is more subtle than a pig. Such an individual is not easy to find.

It was, however, in the heat of these three things, the decline of his merely destructive realism, the discovery of Nietzsche, and the abandonment of the idea of a progressive education of mankind, that he attempted what is not necessarily his best, but certainly his most important work. The two things are by no means necessarily the same. The most important work of Milton is Paradise Lost; his best work is Lycidas. There are other places in which Shaw's argument is more fascinating or his wit more startling than in _Man and Superman;_ there are other plays that he has made more brilliant. But I am sure that there is no other play that he wished to make more brilliant. I will not say that he is in this case more serious than elsewhere; for the word serious is a double-meaning and double-dealing word, a traitor in the dictionary. It sometimes means solemn, and it sometimes means sincere. A very short experience of private and public life will be enough to prove that the most solemn people are generally the most insincere. A somewhat more delicate and detailed consideration will show also that the most sincere men are generally not solemn; and of these is Bernard Shaw. But if we use the word serious in the old and Latin sense of the word "grave," which means weighty or valid, full of substance, then we may say without any hesitation that this is the most serious play of the most serious man alive.

The outline of the play is, I suppose, by this time sufficiently well known. It has two main philosophic motives. The first is that what he calls the life-force (the old infidels called it Nature, which seems a neater word, and nobody knows the meaning of either of them) desires above all things to make suitable marriages, to produce a purer and prouder race, or eventually to produce a Superman. The second is that in this effecting of racial marriages the woman is a more conscious agent than the man. In short, that woman disposes a long time before man proposes. In this play, therefore, woman is made the pursuer and man the pursued. It cannot be denied, I think, that in this matter Shaw is handicapped by his habitual hardness of touch, by his lack of sympathy with the romance of which he writes, and to a certain extent even by his own integrity and right conscience. Whether the man hunts the woman or the woman the man, at least it should be a splendid pagan hunt; but Shaw is not a sporting man. Nor is he a pagan, but a Puritan. He cannot recover the impartiality of paganism which allowed Diana to propose to Endymion without thinking any the worse of her. The result is that while he makes Anne, the woman who marries his hero, a really powerful and convincing woman, he can only do it by making her a highly objectionable woman. She is a liar and a bully, not from sudden fear or excruciating dilemma; she is a liar and a bully in grain; she has no truth or magnanimity in her. The more we know that she is real, the more we know that she is vile. In short, Bernard Shaw is still haunted with his old impotence of the unromantic writer; he cannot imagine the main motives of human life from the inside. We are convinced successfully that Anne wishes to marry Tanner, but in the very process we lose all power of conceiving why Tanner should ever consent to marry Anne. A writer with a more romantic strain in him might have imagined a woman choosing her lover without shamelessness and magnetising him without fraud. Even if the first movement were feminine, it need hardly be a movement like this. In truth, of course, the two sexes have their two methods of attraction, and in some of the happiest cases they are almost simultaneous. But even on the most cynical showing they need not be mixed up. It is one thing to say that the mousetrap is not there by accident. It is another to say (in the face of ocular experience) that the mousetrap runs after the mouse.

But whenever Shaw shows the Puritan hardness or even the Puritan cheapness, he shows something also of the Puritan nobility, of the idea that sacrifice is really a frivolity in the face of a great purpose. The reasonableness of Calvin and his followers will by the mercy of heaven be at last washed away; but their unreasonableness will remain an eternal splendour. Long after we have let drop the fancy that Protestantism was rational it will be its glory that it was fanatical. So it is with Shaw. To make Anne a real woman, even a dangerous woman, he would need to be something stranger and softer than Bernard Shaw. But though I always argue with him whenever he argues, I confess that he always conquers me in the one or two moments when he is emotional.

There is one really noble moment when Anne offers for all her cynical husband-hunting the only defence that is really great enough to cover it. "It will not be all happiness for me. Perhaps death." And the man rises also at that real crisis, saying, "Oh, that clutch holds and hurts. What have you grasped in me? Is there a father's heart as well as a mother's?" That seems to me actually great; I do not like either of the characters an atom more than formerly; but I can see shining and shaking through them at that instant the splendour of the God that made them and of the image of God who wrote their story.

A logician is like a liar in many respects, but chiefly in the fact that he should have a good memory. That cutting and inquisitive style which Bernard Shaw has always adopted carries with it an inevitable criticism. And it cannot be denied that this new theory of the supreme importance of sound sexual union, wrought by any means, is hard logically to reconcile with Shaw's old diatribes against sentimentalism and operatic romance. If Nature wishes primarily to entrap us into sexual union, then all the means of sexual attraction, even the most maudlin or theatrical, are justified at one stroke. The guitar of the troubadour is as practical as the plough-share of the husbandman. The waltz in the ballroom is as serious as the debate in the parish council. The justification of Anne, as the potential mother of Superman, is really the justification of all the humbugs and sentimentalists whom Shaw had been denouncing as a dramatic critic and as a dramatist since the beginning of his career. It was to no purpose that the earlier Bernard Shaw said that romance was all moonshine. The moonshine that ripens love is now as practical as the sunshine that ripens corn. It was vain to say that sexual chivalry was all rot; it might be as rotten as manure--and also as fertile. It is vain to call first love a fiction; it may be as fictitious as the ink of the cuttle or the doubling of the hare; as fictitious, as efficient, and as indispensable. It is vain to call it a self-deception; Schopenhauer said that all existence was a self-deception; and Shaw's only further comment seems to be that it is right to be deceived. To Man and Superman, as to all his plays, the author attaches a most fascinating preface at the beginning. But I really think that he ought also to attach a hearty apology at the end; an apology to all the minor dramatists or preposterous actors whom he had cursed for romanticism in his youth. Whenever he objected to an actress for ogling she might reasonably reply, "But this is how I support my friend Anne in her sublime evolutionary effort." Whenever he laughed at an old-fashioned actor for ranting, the actor might answer, "My exaggeration is not more absurd than the tail of a peacock or the swagger of a cock; it is the way I preach the great fruitful lie of the life-force that I am a very fine fellow." We have remarked the end of Shaw's campaign in favour of progress. This ought really to have been the end of his campaign against romance. All the tricks of love that he called artificial become natural; because they become Nature. All the lies of love become truths; indeed they become the Truth.

The minor things of the play contain some thunderbolts of good thinking. Throughout this brief study I have deliberately not dwelt upon mere wit, because in anything of Shaw's that may be taken for granted. It is enough to say that this play which is full of his most serious quality is as full as any of his minor sort of success. In a more solid sense two important facts stand out: the first is the character of the young American; the other is the character of Straker, the chauffeur. In these Shaw has realised and made vivid two most important facts. First, that America is not intellectually a go-ahead country, but both for good and evil an old-fashioned one. It is full of stale culture and ancestral simplicity, just as Shaw's young millionaire quotes Macaulay and piously worships his wife. Second, he has pointed out in the character of Straker that there has arisen in our midst a new class that has education without breeding. Straker is the man who has ousted the hansom-cabman, having neither his coarseness nor his kindliness. Great sociological credit is due to the man who has first clearly observed that Straker has appeared. How anybody can profess for a moment to be glad that he has appeared, I do not attempt to conjecture.

Appended to the play is an entertaining though somewhat mysterious document called "The Revolutionist's Handbook." It contains many very sound remarks; this, for example, which I cannot too much applaud: "If you hit your child, be sure that you hit him in anger." If that principle had been properly understood, we should have had less of Shaw's sociological friends and their meddling with the habits and instincts of the poor. But among the fragments of advice also occurs the following suggestive and even alluring remark: "Every man over forty is a scoundrel." On the first personal opportunity I asked the author of this remarkable axiom what it meant. I gathered that what it really meant was something like this: that every man over forty had been all the essential use that he was likely to be, and was therefore in a manner a parasite. It is gratifying to reflect that Bernard Shaw has sufficiently answered his own epigram by continuing to pour out treasures both of truth and folly long after this allotted time. But if the epigram might be interpreted in a rather looser style as meaning that past a certain point a man's work takes on its final character and does not greatly change the nature of its merits, it may certainly be said that with Man and Superman, Shaw reaches that stage. The two plays that have followed it, though of very great interest in themselves, do not require any revaluation of, or indeed any addition to, our summary of his genius and success. They are both in a sense casts back to his primary energies; the first in a controversial and the second in a technical sense. Neither need prevent our saying that the moment when John Tanner and Anne agree that it is doom for him and death for her and life only for the thing unborn, is the peak of his utterance as a prophet.

The two important plays that he has since given us are The Doctor's Dilemma and Getting Married. The first is as regards its most amusing and effective elements a throw-back to his old game of guying the men of science. It was a very good game, and he was an admirable player. The actual story of the Doctor's Dilemma itself seems to me less poignant and important than the things with which Shaw had lately been dealing. First of all, as has been said, Shaw has neither the kind of justice nor the kind of weakness that goes to make a true problem. We cannot feel the Doctor's Dilemma, because we cannot really fancy Bernard Shaw being in a dilemma. His mind is both fond of abruptness and fond of finality; he always makes up his mind when he knows the facts and sometimes before. Moreover, this particular problem (though Shaw is certainly, as we shall see, nearer to pure doubt about it than about anything else) does not strike the critic as being such an exasperating problem after all. An artist of vast power and promise, who is also a scamp of vast profligacy and treachery, has a chance of life if specially treated for a special disease. The modern doctors (and even the modern dramatist) are in doubt whether he should be specially favoured because he is aesthetically important or specially disregarded because he is ethically anti-social. They see-saw between the two despicable modern doctrines, one that geniuses should be worshipped like idols and the other that criminals should be merely wiped out like germs. That both clever men and bad men ought to be treated like men does not seem to occur to them. As a matter of fact, in these affairs of life and death one never does think of such distinctions. Nobody does shout out at sea, "Bad citizen over-board!" I should recommend the doctor in his dilemma to do exactly what I am sure any decent doctor would do without any dilemma at all: to treat the man simply as a man, and give him no more and no less favour than he would to anybody else. In short, I am sure a practical physician would drop all these visionary, unworkable modern dreams about type and criminology and go back to the plain business-like facts of the French Revolution and the Rights of Man.

The other play, Getting Married, is a point in Shaw's career, but only as a play, not, as usual, as a heresy. It is nothing but a conversation about marriage and one cannot agree or disagree with the view of marriage, because all views are given which are held by anybody, and some (I should think) which are held by nobody. But its technical quality is of some importance in the life of its author. It is worth consideration as a play, because it is not a play at all. It marks the culmination and completeness of that victory of Bernard Shaw over the British public, or rather over their official representatives, of which I have spoken. Shaw had fought a long fight with business men, those incredible people, who assured him that it was useless to have wit without murders, and that a good joke, which is the most popular thing everywhere else, was quite unsalable in the theatrical world. In spite of this he had conquered by his wit and his good dialogue; and by the time of which we now speak he was victorious and secure. All his plays were being produced as a matter of course in England and as a matter of the fiercest fashion and enthusiasm in America and Germany. No one who knows the nature of the man will doubt that under such circumstances his first act would be to produce his wit naked and unashamed. He had been told that he could not support a slight play by mere dialogue. He therefore promptly produced mere dialogue without the slightest play for it to support. Getting Married is no more a play than Cicero's dialogue De Amicti? and not half so much a play as Wilson's Noctes Ambrosianae. But though it is not a play, it was played, and played successfully. Everyone who went into the theatre felt that he was only eavesdropping at an accidental conversation. But the conversation was so sparkling and sensible that he went on eavesdropping. This, I think, as it is the final play of Shaw, is also, and fitly, his final triumph. He is a good dramatist and sometimes even a great dramatist. But the occasions when we get glimpses of him as really a great man are on these occasions when he is utterly undramatic.

From first to last Bernard Shaw has been nothing but a conversationalist. It is not a slur to say so; Socrates was one, and even Christ Himself. He differs from that divine and that human prototype in the fact that, like most modern people, he does to some extent talk in order to find out what he thinks; whereas they knew it beforehand. But he has the virtues that go with the talkative man; one of which is humility. You will hardly ever find a really proud man talkative; he is afraid of talking too much. Bernard Shaw offered himself to the world with only one great qualification, that he could talk honestly and well. He did not speak; he talked to a crowd. He did not write; he talked to a typewriter. He did not really construct a play; he talked through ten mouths or masks instead of through one. His literary power and progress began in casual conversations-- and it seems to me supremely right that it should end in one great and casual conversation. His last play is nothing but garrulous talking, that great thing called gossip. And I am happy to say that the play has been as efficient and successful as talk and gossip have always been among the children of men.

Of his life in these later years I have made no pretence of telling even the little that there is to tell. Those who regard him as a mere self-advertising egotist may be surprised to hear that there is perhaps no man of whose private life less could be positively said by an outsider. Even those who know him can make little but a conjecture of what has lain behind this splendid stretch of intellectual self-expression; I only make my conjecture like the rest. I think that the first great turning-point in Shaw's life (after the early things of which I have spoken, the taint of drink in the teetotal home, or the first fight with poverty) was the deadly illness which fell upon him, at the end of his first flashing career as a Saturday Reviewer. I know it would goad Shaw to madness to suggest that sickness could have softened him. That is why I suggest it. But I say for his comfort that I think it hardened him also; if that can be called hardening which is only the strengthening of our souls to meet some dreadful reality. At least it is certain that the larger spiritual ambitions, the desire to find a faith and found a church, come after that time. I also mention it because there is hardly anything else to mention; his life is singularly free from landmarks, while his literature is so oddly full of surprises. His marriage to Miss Payne-Townsend, which occurred not long after his illness, was one of those quite successful things which are utterly silent. The placidity of his married life may be sufficiently indicated by saying that (as far as I can make out) the most important events in it were rows about the Executive of the Fabian Society. If such ripples do not express a still and lake-like life, I do not know what would. Honestly, the only thing in his later career that can be called an event is the stand made by Shaw at the Fabians against the sudden assault of Mr. H. G. Wells, which, after scenes of splendid exasperations, ended in Wells' resignation. There was another slight ruffling of the calm when Bernard Shaw said some quite sensible things about Sir Henry Irving. But on the whole we confront the composure of one who has come into his own.

The method of his life has remained mostly unchanged. And there is a great deal of method in his life; I can hear some people murmuring something about method in his madness. He is not only neat and business-like; but, unlike some literary men I know, does not conceal the fact. Having all the talents proper to an author, he delights to prove that he has also all the talents proper to a publisher; or even to a publisher's clerk. Though many looking at his light brown clothes would call him a Bohemian, he really hates and despises Bohemianism; in the sense that he hates and despises disorder and uncleanness and irresponsibility. All that part of him is peculiarly normal and efficient. He gives good advice; he always answers letters, and answers them in a decisive and very legible hand. He has said himself that the only educational art that he thinks important is that of being able to jump off tram-cars at the proper moment. Though a rigid vegetarian, he is quite regular and rational in his meals; and though he detests sport, he takes quite sufficient exercise. While he has always made a mock of science in theory, he is by nature prone to meddle with it in practice. He is fond of photographing, and even more fond of being photographed. He maintained (in one of his moments of mad modernity) that photography was a finer thing than portrait-painting, more exquisite and more imaginative; he urged the characteristic argument that none of his own photographs were like each other or like him. But he would certainly wash the chemicals off his hands the instant after an experiment; just as he would wash the blood off his hands the instant after a Socialist massacre. He cannot endure stains or accretions; he is of that temperament which feels tradition itself to be a coat of dust; whose temptation it is to feel nothing but a sort of foul accumulation or living disease even in the creeper upon the cottage or the moss upon the grave. So thoroughly are his tastes those of the civilised modern man that if it had not been for the fire in him of justice and anger he might have been the most trim and modern among the millions whom he shocks: and his bicycle and brown hat have been no menace in Brixton. But God sent among those suburbans one who was a prophet as well as a sanitary inspector. He had every qualification for living in a villa-- except the necessary indifference to his brethren living in pigsties. But for the small fact that he hates with a sickening hatred the hypocrisy and class cruelty, he would really accept and admire the bathroom and the bicycle and asbestos-stove, having no memory of rivers or of roaring fires. In these things, like Mr. Straker, he is the New Man. But for his great soul he might have accepted modern civilisation; it was a wonderful escape. This man whom men so foolishly call crazy and anarchic has really a dangerous affinity to the fourth-rate perfections of our provincial and Protestant civilisation. He might even have been respectable if he had had less self-respect.

His fulfilled fame and this tone of repose and reason in his life, together with the large circle of his private kindness and the regard of his fellow-artists, should permit us to end the record in a tone of almost patriarchal quiet. If I wished to complete such a picture I could add many touches: that he has consented to wear evening dress; that he has supported the Times Book Club; and that his beard has turned grey; the last to his regret, as he wanted it to remain red till they had completed colour-photography. He can mix with the most conservative statesmen; his tone grows continuously more gentle in the matter of religion. It would be easy to end with the lion lying down with the lamb, the wild Irishman tamed or taming everybody, Shaw reconciled to the British public as the British public is certainly largely reconciled to Shaw.

But as I put these last papers together, having finished this rude study, I hear a piece of news. His latest play, _The Showing Up of Blanco Posnet,_ has been forbidden by the Censor. As far as I can discover, it has been forbidden because one of the characters professes a belief in God and states his conviction that God has got him. This is wholesome; this is like one crack of thunder in a clear sky. Not so easily does the prince of this world forgive. Shaw's religious training and instinct is not mine, but in all honest religion there is something that is hateful to the prosperous compromise of our time.

You are free in our time to say that God does not exist; you are free to say that He exists and is evil; you are free to say (like poor old Renan) that He would like to exist if He could. You may talk of God as a metaphor or a mystification; you may water Him down with gallons of long words, or boil Him to the rags of metaphysics; and it is not merely that nobody punishes, but nobody protests. But if you speak of God as a fact, as a thing like a tiger, as a reason for changing one's conduct, then the modern world will stop you somehow if it can. We are long past talking about whether an unbeliever should be punished for being irreverent. It is now thought irreverent to be a believer. I end where I began: it is the old Puritan in Shaw that jars the modern world like an electric shock. That vision with which I meant to end, that vision of culture and common-sense, of red brick and brown flannel, of the modern clerk broadened enough to embrace Shaw and Shaw softened enough to embrace the clerk, all that vision of a new London begins to fade and alter. The red brick begins to burn red-hot; and the smoke from all the chimneys has a strange smell. I find myself back in the fumes in which I started. . . . Perhaps I have been misled by small modernities. Perhaps what I have called fastidiousness is a divine fear. Perhaps what I have called coldness is a predestinate and ancient endurance. The vision of the Fabian villas grows fainter and fainter, until I see only a void place across which runs Bunyan's Pilgrim with his fingers in his ears.

Bernard Shaw has occupied much of his life in trying to elude his followers. The fox has enthusiastic followers, and Shaw seems to regard his in much the same way. This man whom men accuse of bidding for applause seems to me to shrink even from assent. If you agree with Shaw he is very likely to contradict you; I have contradicted Shaw throughout, that is why I come at last almost to agree with him. His critics have accused him of vulgar self-advertisement; in his relation to his followers he seems to me rather marked with a sort of mad modesty. He seems to wish to fly from agreement, to have as few followers as possible. All this reaches back, I think, to the three roots from which this meditation grew. It is partly the mere impatience and irony of the Irishman. It is party the thought of the Calvinist that the host of God should be thinned rather than thronged; that Gideon must reject soldiers rather than recruit them. And it is partly, alas, the unhappy Progressive trying to be in front of his own religion, trying to destroy his own idol and even to desecrate his own tomb. But from whatever causes, this furious escape from popularity has involved Shaw in some perversities and refinements which are almost mere insincerities, and which make it necessary to disentangle the good he has done from the evil in this dazzling course. I will attempt some summary by stating the three things in which his influence seems to me thoroughly good and the three in which it seems bad. But for the pleasure of ending on the finer note I will speak first of those that seem bad.

The primary respect in which Shaw has been a bad influence is that he has encouraged fastidiousness. He has made men dainty about their moral meals. This is indeed the root of his whole objection to romance. Many people have objected to romance for being too airy and exquisite. Shaw objects to romance for being too rank and coarse. Many have despised romance because it is unreal; Shaw really hates it because it is a great deal too real. Shaw dislikes romance as he dislikes beef and beer, raw brandy or raw beefsteaks. Romance is too masculine for his taste. You will find throughout his criticisms, amid all their truth, their wild justice or pungent impartiality, a curious undercurrent of prejudice upon one point: the preference for the refined rather than the rude or ugly. Thus he will dislike a joke because it is coarse without asking if it is really immoral. He objects to a man sitting down on his hat, whereas the austere moralist should only object to his sitting down on someone else's hat. This sensibility is barren because it is universal. It is useless to object to man being made ridiculous. Man is born ridiculous, as can easily be seen if you look at him soon after he is born. It is grotesque to drink beer, but it is equally grotesque to drink soda-water; the grotesqueness lies in the act of filling yourself like a bottle through a hole. It is undignified to walk with a drunken stagger; but it is fairly undignified to walk at all, for all walking is a sort of balancing, and there is always in the human being something of a quadruped on its hind legs. I do not say he would be more dignified if he went on all fours; I do not know that he ever is dignified except when he is dead. We shall not be refined till we are refined into dust. Of course it is only because he is not wholly an animal that man sees he is a rum animal; and if man on his hind legs is in an artificial attitude, it is only because, like a dog, he is begging or saying thank you.

Everything important is in that sense absurd from the grave baby to the grinning skull; everything practical is a practical joke. But throughout Shaw's comedies, curiously enough, there is a certain kicking against this great doom of laughter. For instance, it is the first duty of a man who is in love to make a fool of himself; but Shaw's heroes always seem to flinch from this, and attempt, in airy, philosophic revenge, to make a fool of the woman first. The attempts of Valentine and Charteris to divide their perceptions from their desires, and tell the woman she is worthless even while trying to win her, are sometimes almost torturing to watch; it is like seeing a man trying to play a different tune with each hand. I fancy this agony is not only in the spectator, but in the dramatist as well. It is Bernard Shaw struggling with his reluctance to do anything so ridiculous as make a proposal. For there are two types of great humorist: those who love to see a man absurd and those who hate to see him absurd. Of the first kind are Rabelais and Dickens; of the second kind are Swift and Bernard Shaw.

So far as Shaw has spread or helped a certain modern reluctance or mauvaise honte in these grand and grotesque functions of man I think he has definitely done harm. He has much influence among the young men; but it is not an influence in the direction of keeping them young. One cannot imagine him inspiring any of his followers to write a war-song or a drinking-song or a love-song, the three forms of human utterance which come next in nobility to a prayer. It may seem odd to say that the net effect of a man so apparently impudent will be to make men shy. But it is certainly the truth. Shyness is always the sign of a divided soul; a man is shy because he somehow thinks his position at once despicable and important. If he were without humility he would not care; and if he were without pride he would not care. Now the main purpose of Shaw's theoretic teaching is to declare that we ought to fulfil these great functions of life, that we ought to eat and drink and love. But the main tendency of his habitual criticism is to suggest that all the sentiments, professions, and postures of these things are not only comic but even contemptibly comic, follies and almost frauds. The result would seem to be that a race of young men may arise who do all these things, but do them awkwardly. That which was of old a free and hilarious function becomes an important and embarrassing necessity. Let us endure all the pagan pleasures with a Christian patience. Let us eat, drink, and be serious.

The second of the two points on which I think Shaw has done definite harm is this: that he has (not always or even as a rule intentionally) increased that anarchy of thought which is always the destruction of thought. Much of his early writing has encouraged among the modern youth that most pestilent of all popular tricks and fallacies; what is called the argument of progress. I mean this kind of thing. Previous ages were often, alas, aristocratic in politics or clericalist in religion; but they were always democratic in philosophy; they appealed to man, not to particular men. And if most men were against an idea, that was so far against it. But nowadays that most men are against a thing is thought to be in its favour; it is vaguely supposed to show that some day most men will be for it. If a man says that cows are reptiles, or that Bacon wrote Shakespeare, he can always quote the contempt of his contemporaries as in some mysterious way proving the complete conversion of posterity. The objections to this theory scarcely need any elaborate indication. The final objection to it is that it amounts to this: say anything, however idiotic, and you are in advance of your age. This kind of stuff must be stopped. The sort of democrat who appeals to the babe unborn must be classed with the sort of aristocrat who appeals to his deceased great-grandfather. Both should be sharply reminded that they are appealing to individuals whom they well know to be at a disadvantage in the matter of prompt and witty reply. Now although Bernard Shaw has survived this simple confusion, he has in his time greatly contributed to it. If there is, for instance, one thing that is really rare in Shaw it is hesitation. He makes up his mind quicker than a calculating boy or a county magistrate. Yet on this subject of the next change in ethics he has felt hesitation, and being a strictly honest man has expressed it.

"I know no harder practical question than how much selfishness one ought to stand from a gifted person for the sake of his gifts or on the chance of his being right in the long run. The Superman will certainly come like a thief in the night, and be shot at accordingly; but we cannot leave our property wholly undefended on that account. On the other hand, we cannot ask the Superman simply to add a higher set of virtues to current respectable morals; for he is undoubtedly going to empty a good deal of respectable morality out like so much dirty water, and replace it by new and strange customs, shedding old obligations and accepting new and heavier ones. Every step of his progress must horrify conventional people; and if it were possible for even the most superior man to march ahead all the time, every pioneer of the march towards the Superman would be crucified."

When the most emphatic man alive, a man unmatched in violent precision of statement, speaks with such avowed vagueness and doubt as this, it is no wonder if all his more weak-minded followers are in a mere whirlpool of uncritical and unmeaning innovation. If the superior person will be apparently criminal, the most probable result is simply that the criminal person will think himself superior. A very slight knowledge of human nature is required in the matter. If the Superman may possibly be a thief, you may bet your boots that the next thief will be a Superman. But indeed the Supermen (of whom I have met many) have generally been more weak in the head than in the moral conduct; they have simply offered the first fancy which occupied their minds as the new morality. I fear that Shaw had a way of encouraging these follies. It is obvious from the passage I have quoted that he has no way of restraining them.

The truth is that all feeble spirits naturally live in the future, because it is featureless; it is a soft job; you can make it what you like. The next age is blank, and I can paint it freely with my favourite colour. It requires real courage to face the past, because the past is full of facts which cannot be got over; of men certainly wiser than we and of things done which we could not do. I know I cannot write a poem as good as Lycidas. But it is always easy to say that the particular sort of poetry I can write will be the poetry of the future.

This I call the second evil influence of Shaw: that he has encouraged many to throw themselves for justification upon the shapeless and the unknown. In this, though courageous himself, he has encouraged cowards, and though sincere himself, has helped a mean escape. The third evil in his influence can, I think, be much more shortly dealt with. He has to a very slight extent, but still perceptibly, encouraged a kind of charlatanism of utterance among those who possess his Irish impudence without his Irish virtue. For instance, his amusing trick of self-praise is perfectly hearty and humorous in him; nay, it is even humble; for to confess vanity is itself humble. All that is the matter with the proud is that they will not admit that they are vain. Therefore when Shaw says that he alone is able to write such and such admirable work, or that he has just utterly wiped out some celebrated opponent, I for one never feel anything offensive in the tone, but, indeed, only the unmistakable intonation of a friend's voice. But I have noticed among younger, harder, and much shallower men a certain disposition to ape this insolent ease and certitude, and that without any fundamental frankness or mirth. So far the influence is bad. Egoism can be learnt as a lesson like any other "ism." It is not so easy to learn an Irish accent or a good temper. In its lower forms the thing becomes a most unmilitary trick of announcing the victory before one has gained it.

When one has said those three things, one has said, I think, all that can be said by way of blaming Bernard Shaw. It is significant that he was never blamed for any of these things by the Censor. Such censures as the attitude of that official involves may be dismissed with a very light sort of disdain. To represent Shaw as profane or provocatively indecent is not a matter for discussion at all; it is a disgusting criminal libel upon a particularly respectable gentleman of the middle classes, of refined tastes and somewhat Puritanical views. But while the negative defence of Shaw is easy, the just praise of him is almost as complex as it is necessary; and I shall devote the last few pages of this book to a triad corresponding to the last one--to the three important elements in which the work of Shaw has been good as well as great.

In the first place, and quite apart from all particular theories, the world owes thanks to Bernard Shaw for having combined being intelligent with being intelligible. He has popularised philosophy, or rather he has re-popularised it, for philosophy is always popular, except in peculiarly corrupt and oligarchic ages like our own. We have passed the age of the demagogue, the man who has little to say and says it loud. We have come to the age of the mystagogue or don, the man who has nothing to say, but says it softly and impressively in an indistinct whisper. After all, short words must mean something, even if they mean filth or lies; but long words may sometimes mean literally nothing, especially if they are used (as they mostly are in modern books and magazine articles) to balance and modify each other. A plain figure 4, scrawled in chalk anywhere, must always mean something; it must always mean $2 + 2$. But the most enormous and mysterious algebraic equation, full of letters, brackets, and fractions, may all cancel out at last and be equal to nothing. When a demagogue says to a mob, "There is the Bank of England, why shouldn't you have some of that money?" he says something which is at least as honest and intelligible as the figure 4. When a writer in the Times remarks, "We must raise the economic efficiency of the masses without diverting anything from those classes which represent the national prosperity and refinement," then his equation cancels out; in a literal and logical sense his remark amounts to nothing.

There are two kinds of charlatans or people called quacks to-day. The power of the first is that he advertises--and cures. The power of the second is that though he is not learned enough to cure he is much too learned to advertise. The former give away their dignity with a pound of tea; the latter are paid a pound of tea merely for being dignified. I think them the worse quacks of the two. Shaw is certainly of the other sort. Dickens, another man who was great enough to be a demagogue (and greater than Shaw because more heartily a demagogue), puts for ever the true difference between the demagogue and the mystagogue in Dr. Marigold: "Except that we're cheap-jacks and they're dear-jacks, I don't see any difference between us." Bernard Shaw is a great cheap-jack, with plenty of patter and I dare say plenty of nonsense, but with this also (which is not wholly unimportant), with goods to sell. People accuse such a man of self-advertisement. But at least the cheap-jack does advertise his wares, whereas the don or dear-jack advertises nothing except himself. His very silence, nay his very sterility, are supposed to be marks of the richness of his erudition. He is too learned to teach, and sometimes too wise even to talk. St. Thomas Aquinas said: "In auctore auctoritas." But there is more than one man at Oxford or Cambridge who is considered an authority because he has never been an author.

Against all this mystification both of silence and verbosity Shaw has been a splendid and smashing protest. He has stood up for the fact that philosophy is not the concern of those who pass through Divinity and Greats, but of those who pass through birth and death. Nearly all the most awful and abstruse statements can be put in words of one syllable, from "A child is born" to "A soul is damned." If the ordinary man may not discuss existence, why should he be asked to conduct it? About concrete matters indeed one naturally appeals to an oligarchy or select class. For information about Lapland I go to an aristocracy of Laplanders; for the ways of rabbits to an aristocracy of naturalists or, preferably, an aristocracy of poachers. But only mankind itself can bear witness to the abstract first principles of mankind, and in matters of theory I would always consult the mob. Only the mass of men, for instance, have authority to say whether life is good. Whether life is good is an especially mystical and delicate question, and, like all such questions, is asked in words of one syllable. It is also answered in words of one syllable, and Bernard Shaw (as also mankind) answers "yes."

This plain, pugnacious style of Shaw has greatly clarified all controversies. He has slain the polysyllable, that huge and slimy centipede which has sprawled over all the valleys of England like the "loathly worm" who was slain by the ancient knight. He does not think that difficult questions will be made simpler by using difficult words about them. He has achieved the admirable work, never to be mentioned without gratitude, of discussing Evolution without mentioning it. The good work is of course more evident in the case of philosophy than any other region; because the case of philosophy was a crying one. It was really preposterous that the things most carefully reserved for the study of two or three men should actually be the things common to all men. It was absurd that certain men should be experts on the special subject of everything. But he stood for much the same spirit and style in other matters; in economics, for example. There never has been a better popular economist; one more lucid, entertaining, consistent, and essentially exact. The very comicality of his examples makes them and their argument stick in the mind; as in the case I remember in which he said that the big shops had now to please everybody, and were not entirely dependent on the lady who sails in "to order four governesses and five grand pianos." He is always preaching collectivism; yet he does not very often name it. He does not talk about collectivism, but about cash; of which the populace feel a much more definite need. He talks about cheese, boots, perambulators, and how people are really to live. For him economics really means housekeeping, as it does in Greek. His difference from the orthodox economists, like most of his differences, is very different from the attacks made by the main body of Socialists. The old Manchester economists are generally attacked for being too gross and material. Shaw really attacks them for not being gross or material enough. He thinks that they hide themselves behind long words, remote hypotheses or unreal generalisations. When the orthodox economist begins with his correct and primary formula, "Suppose there is a Man on an Island--" Shaw is apt to interrupt him sharply, saying, "There is a Man in the Street."

The second phase of the man's really fruitful efficacy is in a sense the converse of this. He has improved philosophic discussions by making them more popular. But he has also improved popular amusements by making them more philosophic. And by more philosophic I do not mean duller, but funnier; that is more varied. All real fun is in cosmic contrasts, which involve a view of the cosmos. But I know that this second strength in Shaw is really difficult to state and must be approached by explanations and even by eliminations. Let me say at once that I think nothing of Shaw or anybody else merely for playing the daring sceptic. I do not think he has done any good or even achieved any effect simply by asking startling questions. It is possible that there have been ages so sluggish or automatic that anything that woke them up at all was a good thing. It is sufficient to be certain that ours is not such an age. We do not need waking up; rather we suffer from insomnia, with all its results of fear and exaggeration and frightful waking dreams. The modern mind is not a donkey which wants kicking to make it go on. The modern mind is more like a motor-car on a lonely road which two amateur motorists have been just clever enough to take to pieces, but are not quite clever enough to put together again. Under these circumstances kicking the car has never been found by the best experts to be effective. No one, therefore, does any good to our age merely by asking questions--unless he can answer the questions. Asking questions is already the fashionable and aristocratic sport which has brought most of us into the bankruptcy court. The note of our age is a note of interrogation. And the final point is so plain; no sceptical philosopher can ask any questions that may not equally be asked by a tired child on a hot afternoon. "Am I a boy?--Why am I a boy?--Why aren't I a chair?--What is a chair?" A child will sometimes ask questions of this sort for two hours. And the philosophers of Protestant Europe have asked them for two hundred years.

If that were all that I meant by Shaw making men more philosophic, I should put it not among his good influences but his bad. He did do that to some extent; and so far he is bad. But there is a much bigger and better sense in which he has been a philosopher. He has brought back into English drama all the streams of fact or tendency which are commonly called undramatic. They were there in Shakespeare's time; but they have scarcely been there since until Shaw. I mean that Shakespeare, being interested in everything, put everything into a play. If he had lately been thinking about the irony and even contradiction confronting us in self-preservation and suicide, he put it all into Hamlet. If he was annoyed by some passing boom in theatrical babies he put that into Hamlet too. He would put anything into Hamlet which he really thought was true, from his favourite nursery ballads to his personal (and perhaps unfashionable) conviction of the Catholic purgatory. There is no fact that strikes one, I think, about Shakespeare, except the fact of how dramatic he could be, so much as the fact of how undramatic he could be.

In this great sense Shaw has brought philosophy back into drama-- philosophy in the sense of a certain freedom of the mind. This is not a freedom to think what one likes (which is absurd, for one can only think what one thinks); it is a freedom to think about what one likes, which is quite a different thing and the spring of all thought. Shakespeare (in a weak moment, I think) said that all the world is a stage. But Shakespeare acted on the much finer principle that a stage is all the world. So there are in all Bernard Shaw's plays patches of what people would call essentially undramatic stuff, which the dramatist puts in because he is honest and would rather prove his case than succeed with his play. Shaw has brought back into English drama that Shakespearian universality which, if you like, you can call Shakespearian irrelevance. Perhaps a better definition than either is a habit of thinking the truth worth telling even when you meet it by accident. In Shaw's plays one meets an incredible number of truths by accident.

To be up to date is a paltry ambition except in an almanac, and Shaw has sometimes talked this almanac philosophy. Nevertheless there is a real sense in which the phrase may be wisely used, and that is in cases where some stereotyped version of what is happening hides what is really happening from our eyes. Thus, for instance, newspapers are never up to date. The men who write leading articles are always behind the times, because they are in a hurry. They are forced to fall back on their old-fashioned view of things; they have no time to fashion a new one. Everything that is done in a hurry is certain to be antiquated; that is why modern industrial civilisation bears so curious a resemblance to barbarism. Thus when newspapers say that the Times is a solemn old Tory paper, they are out of date; their talk is behind the talk in Fleet Street. Thus when newspapers say that Christian dogmas are crumbling, they are out of date; their talk is behind the talk in public-houses. Now in this sense Shaw has kept in a really stirring sense up to date. He has introduced into the theatre the things that no one else had introduced into a theatre--the things in the street outside. The theatre is a sort of thing which proudly sends a hansom-cab across the stage as Realism, while everybody outside is whistling for motor-cabs.

Consider in this respect how many and fine have been Shaw's intrusions into the theatre with the things that were really going on. Daily papers and daily matinees were still gravely explaining how much modern war depended on gunpowder. Arms and the Man explained how much modern war depends on chocolate. Every play and paper described the Vicar who was a mild Conservative. Candida caught hold of the modern Vicar who is an advanced Socialist. Numberless magazine articles and society comedies describe the emancipated woman as new and wild. Only You Never Can Tell was young enough to see that the emancipated woman is already old and respectable. Every comic paper has caricatured the uneducated upstart. Only the author of Man and Superman knew enough about the modern world to caricature the educated upstart--the man Straker who can quote Beaumarchais, though he cannot pronounce him. This is the second real and great work of Shaw--the letting in of the world on to the stage, as the rivers were let in upon the Augean Stable. He has let a little of the Haymarket into the Haymarket Theatre. He has permitted some whispers of the Strand to enter the Strand Theatre. A variety of solutions in philosophy is as silly as it is in arithmetic, but one may be justly proud of a variety of materials for a solution. After Shaw, one may say, there is nothing that cannot be introduced into a play if one can make it decent, amusing, and relevant. The state of a man's health, the religion of his childhood, his ear for music, or his ignorance of cookery can all be made vivid if they have anything to do with the subject. A soldier may mention the commissariat as well as the cavalry; and, better still, a priest may mention theology as well as religion. That is being a philosopher; that is bringing the universe on the stage.

Lastly, he has obliterated the mere cynic. He has been so much more cynical than anyone else for the public good that no one has dared since to be really cynical for anything smaller. The Chinese crackers of the frivolous cynics fail to excite us after the dynamite of the serious and aspiring cynic. Bernard Shaw and I (who are growing grey together) can remember an epoch which many of his followers do not know: an epoch of real pessimism. The years from 1885 to 1898 were like the hours of afternoon in a rich house with large rooms; the hours before tea-time. They believed in nothing except good manners; and the essence of good manners is to conceal a yawn. A yawn may be defined as a silent yell. The power which the young pessimist of that time showed in this direction would have astonished anyone but him. He yawned so wide as to swallow the world. He swallowed the world like an unpleasant pill before retiring to an eternal rest. Now the last and best glory of Shaw is that in the circles where this creature was found, he is not. He has not been killed (I don't know exactly why), but he has actually turned into a Shaw idealist. This is no exaggeration. I meet men who, when I knew them in 1898, were just a little too lazy to destroy the universe. They are now conscious of not being quite worthy to abolish some prison regulations. This destruction and conversion seem to me the mark of something actually great. It is always great to destroy a type without destroying a man. The followers of Shaw are optimists; some of them are so simple as even to use the word. They are sometimes rather pallid optimists, frequently very worried optimists, occasionally, to tell the truth, rather cross optimists: but they [are] not pessimists; they can exult though they cannot laugh. He has at least withered up among them the mere pose of impossibility. Like every great teacher, he has cursed the barren fig-tree. For nothing except that impossibility is really impossible.

* * * *

I know it is all very strange. From the height of eight hundred years ago, or of eight hundred years hence, our age must look incredibly odd. We call the twelfth century ascetic. We call our own time hedonist and full of praise and pleasure. But in the ascetic age the love of life was evident and enormous, so that it had to be restrained. In an hedonist age pleasure has always sunk low, so that it has to be encouraged. How high the sea of human happiness rose in the Middle Ages, we now only know by the colossal walls that they built to keep it in bounds. How low human happiness sank in the twentieth century our children will only know by these extraordinary modern books, which tell people that it is a duty to be cheerful and that life is not so bad after all. Humanity never produces optimists till it has ceased to produce happy men. It is strange to be obliged to impose a holiday like a fast, and to drive men to a banquet with spears. But this shall be written of our time: that when the spirit who denies besieged the last citadel, blaspheming life itself, there were some, there was one especially, whose voice was heard and whose spear was never broken.

THE END

CPSIA information can be obtained at www.ICGtesting.com
Printed in the USA
LVOW01s0839200415

435212LV00048BB/1987/P